Teacher

Hampton-Brown

EDGE

NATIONAL GEOGRAPHIC LEARNING | CENGAGE Learning®

Acknowledgments
Grateful acknowledgment is given to the authors, artists, photographers, museums, publishers, and agents for permission to reprint copyrighted material. Every effort has been made to secure the appropriate permission. If any omissions have been made or if corrections are required, please contact the Publisher.

Photographic Credits
Cover: Ancient Eye, Arches National Park, Utah, USA, Marsel van Oosten. Photograph © Marsel van Oosten/ squiver.com.

For product information and technology asistance, contact us at
Cengage Learning Customer & Sales Support, 1-800-354-9706

For permission to use material from this text or product, submit all requests online at **www.cengage.com/permissions**
Further permissions questions can be emailed to
permissionrequest@cengage.com

National Geographic Learning | Cengage Learning
1 Lower Ragsdale Drive
Building 1, Suite 200
Monterey, CA 93940

Cengage Learning is a leading provider of customized learning solutions with office locations around the globe, including Singapore, the United Kingdom, Australia, Mexico, Brazil, and Japan. Locate your local office at **www.cengage.com/global**.

Visit National Geographic Learning online at **ngl.cengage.com**
Visit our corporate website at **www.cengage.com**

Printed in the USA.
RR Donnelley, Willard, OH

ISBN: 978-12857-34866 (Practice Book)
ISBN: 978-12857-34897 (Practice Book Teacher's Annotated Edition)

ISBN: 978-12857-67321 (Practice Masters)

Printed in the United States of America

13 14 15 16 17 18 19 20 21 22

10 9 8 7 6 5 4 3 2 1

Contents

Contents, *continued*

UNIT 4

UNIT 5

Contents, *continued*

UNIT 7

Grammar: Present Perfect Tense

Grammar: Perfect Tenses

Grammar: Participles and Participial Phrases

Proofreader's Marks

Mark	Meaning	Example
≡	Capitalize.	I love new york city.
/	Do not capitalize.	I'm going shopping at my favorite Store.
⊙	Add a period.	Mr⊙Lopez is our neighbor.
?	Add a question mark.	Where is my black pen?
!	Add an exclamation point.	Look out!
" "	Add quotation marks.	"You are late," said the teacher.
^,	Add a comma.	Amy^, how are you feeling today?
^;	Add a semicolon.	This shirt is nice^; however, that one brings out the color of your eyes.
:	Add a colon.	He wakes up at 6:30 a.m.
—	Add a dash.	Barney—he's my pet dog—has run away.
( )	Add parentheses.	I want to work for the Federal Bureau of Investigation (FBI) .
=	Add a hyphen.	You were born in mid=September, right?
'	Add an apostrophe.	I'm the oldest of five children.
#	Add a space.	She likes him alot.
⁀	Close up a space.	How much home work do you have?
^	Add text.	My keys are ^on the table.
℘	Delete.	I am going too my friend's house.
^ ℘	Change text.	We have ^too to much garbage.
∿	Transpose words, letters.	Did you see thier new car?
(sp)	Spell out.	Today he is turning (16). (sp)
¶	Begin a new paragraph.	"I win!" I shouted.¶ "No, you don't," he said.
(ital) ___	Add italics.	The Spanish word for table is mesa. (ital)
(u/s) ___	Add underlining.	Little Women is one of my favorite books. (u/s)

Name ______________________ Date ____________

1 Are All Sentences the Same?

No. They Have Different Purposes.

Four Kinds of Sentences

1. Make a **statement** to tell something. End with a period.
   Andrea and I are friends. We know each other really well.

2. Ask a **question** to find out something. End with a question mark.
   Do you know Andrea, too? Is she your friend?

3. Use an **exclamation** to express a strong feeling. End with an exclamation point.
   What a surprise this is! Andrea plays hockey! I can't believe it!

4. Give a **command** to tell someone what to do. End with a period. For strong commands, end with an exclamation point.
   Tell me about hockey. Show me your skates. Watch out!

Start every sentence with a capital letter.

Try It

A. Read each sentence. Decide what kind of sentence it is. Write **statement**, **question**, **exclamation**, or **command**. Then write it as another kind of sentence.

Sentences will vary.

1. Andrea is my best friend. statement; Is Andrea my best friend?
2. What a good hockey player she is! exclamation; She is a good hockey player.
3. Is she the star of her team? question; She is the star of her team.
4. Take me to her hockey game. command; Will you take me to her hockey game?

B. These sentences are missing end punctuation. Edit the sentences to add punctuation. Possible responses:

5. I didn't know that Andrea plays hockey.
6. How surprised I was to find out!
7. Why didn't she tell me?
8. Please do not keep secrets from me.
9. What else does Andrea do for fun?
10. I will ask her more about that.

Proofreader's Marks

Add a period:

I learned something new.

Add a question mark:

Did you know about this?

Add an exclamation point:

What a surprise that is!

See all Proofreader's Marks on page ix.

Write It

C. What surprising information have you learned about someone you know? Complete the sentences to tell about it. Make sure you use the correct punctuation.

11. My best friend ______________________________
12. Did you know ______________________________
13. How shocked ______________________________
14. Please tell ______________________________
15. I never knew ______________________________

D. (16–20) What don't your friends know about you? Write at least five sentences. Use a statement, a question, an exclamation, and a command.

____

____

____

____

____

____

Name ______________________ Date ____________

2 What Do You Need for a Sentence?

A Subject and a Predicate

A complete sentence has two parts: the **subject** and the **predicate**.

subject **predicate**

Paula goes to school with Brett.

To find the parts in most sentences, ask yourself:

1. Whom or what is the sentence about? The answer is the **subject**. It may be one word or more than one word.
2. What does the subject do? The answer is the **predicate**. Like the subject, it may be one word or more than one word.

Sentence	Whom or What?	What Does the Subject Do?
Brett needs help in science.	Brett	needs help in science
His friend Paula notices.	His friend Paula	notices

Try It

A. Draw a line from each subject to a predicate to make a sentence. Possible responses:

1. Rosa — looks for her backpack.
2. Her backpack — has her books, homework, and keys in it.
3. A classmate named Rico — helps.
4. He — finds the backpack under a tree.

B. Complete each sentence with a subject or a predicate. Possible responses:

5. The coach teaches me to play basketball.
6. Craig works at the toy store.

7. Martha shares her lunch with me.

8. The new girl makes friends at school.

Write It

C. Answer the questions to tell about people who are your friends. Circle the subjects in your answers. Underline the predicates.

9. Who is one of your friends? One of my friends is ______.

10. What do you and your friend do together? We ______.

11. How does your friend help you? ______

______

D. (12–13) What makes someone a good friend? Write at least two complete sentences. Circle the subjects. Underline the predicates.

______

______

Edit It

E. (14–18) Edit this journal entry. Fill in the five missing subjects or predicates. The first one is done for you. Possible responses:

May 23

Celia has lived next door to me for two years. I ~~N~~ever knew her before. I locked myself out of my house today. The windows and doors were closed. Celia invited me in. I ~~S~~tayed with her until Mom got home. We played board games. Now I have a new friend. I ~~A~~m glad.

Proofreader's Marks

Add text:
She gave me lunch.

Do not capitalize:
We had ~~F~~un.

See all Proofreader's Marks on page ix.

Name ______________________ Date ____________

3 What Is a Sentence About?

The Subject

The **complete subject** can be one word or a phrase of several words. Zoom in on the most important word. Is it a noun? A **noun** is the name of a person, place, thing, or idea.

1. **Joshua** played soccer last winter.
2. An opposing **player** kicked the ball hard.
3. The **ball** flew into Joshua's leg.
4. The **pain** was overwhelming.
5. An **ambulance** took him to the hospital.
6. The **emergency room** was quite busy.

Nouns in the Subject	
Person	Joshua player
Place	emergency room
Thing	ball ambulance
Idea	pain

Try It

A. Write a noun to complete the subject of each sentence about Joshua. Possible responses:

1. The emergency room ___doctor___ took X-rays.
2. Joshua's ___leg___ was broken.
3. Now the unhappy ___boy___ has a cast and crutches.
4. His ___friends___ signed the cast and drew pictures on it.
5. The colorful ___cast___ has to stay on for six weeks.

B. (6–10) Complete the paragraph. Write nouns to complete the subjects. Possible responses:

Joshua's soccer ___team___ felt bad for Joshua. The ___players___ decided to cheer him up by making him dinner. The big potluck ___dinner___ was delicious. Joshua's ___kitchen___ was full of all kinds of food. His friends' ___kindness___ helped Joshua to feel a lot happier.

Write It

C. Suppose you broke your leg and your friends brought you food. Answer the questions to tell how some things would help. Circle the most important noun in the complete subject.

11. What foods would help your bones heal? ______________ would help to ______________.

12. What foods would keep you warm? ______________.

13. What foods would cheer you up? ______________ would help me to feel a lot better.

14. What else would help with your recovery? ______________

D. (15–18) Accidents happen all the time. Write four sentences about accidents and their consequences. Use a different subject in each sentence.

____

____

____

____

____

Edit It

Possible responses:

E. Dear Joshua,

Thank you for visiting me at the hospital today. Your ^mom was very kind to drive you here. That broken ^leg must be a real problem for you. The ^crutches make it hard to get around. The ^nurses thought you did a great job, though. My ^doctor just came in to check on me. He said I can go home soon. I can't wait. The ^hospital is not my favorite place! Your ^grandma can take good care of me at home.

Love,

Grandpa

Proofreader's Marks

Add text: Joshua ^ visited his grandpa at the hospital.

See all Proofreader's Marks on page ix.

Name ______________________________ Date ______________

4 What's the Most Important Word in the Predicate?

The Verb

- The **complete predicate** in a sentence often tells what the subject does. It can be one word or several words. The **verb** shows the action.

  My best friend **invites** me to her house.

  I **decide** to ride my bike.

- Sometimes the predicate tells what the subject has. It uses these **verbs**:

  My bike **has** a flat tire.

  I **have** a kit for patching it.

- Other times, the predicate tells what the subject is or is like. The **verb** is a form of **be**.

  All the tools **are** in my kit.

  My tire **is** not flat anymore.

  I **am** proud of myself!

Try It

A. Write a verb to complete the predicate of each sentence. Possible responses:

1. I ____am____ not that good at fixing things.
2. Usually, I ____call____ my dad for help.
3. This time I ____fix____ my flat tire by myself.
4. Then I ____ride____ to my friend Amy's house.
5. She ____is____ proud of me!
6. My dad ____is____ proud of me, too.
7. I ____have____ more confidence now.

B. (8–13) Complete the paragraph. Write verbs to complete the predicates. Possible responses:

We are in my friend's yard. A lost dog __wanders__ into the yard. The friendly dog __has__ a collar but no license tag. My friend's mom __is__ not home. At first, we __wonder__ what to do. Then we take care of the problem ourselves. We __call__ the police. They eventually __find__ the dog's owner.

Write It

C. Tell about a problem you had and how you solved it. Add predicates to the subjects below. Underline the verb in each predicate.

14. My problem ____________________.

15. To solve my problem, I ____________________.

16. Next, I ____________________.

D. (17–20) When have you surprised yourself by realizing you could do something you thought you couldn't do? Write at least four sentences. Underline the verb in each predicate.

____

____

____

____

____

Edit It

E. (21–26) Edit the paragraph by adding verbs in the predicates. Fix the six mistakes.

Possible responses:

I am on the train on my way to the city. The train car ^has mechanical problems. An announcement ^asks passengers to leave the car. Some of the older passengers ^are confused. How will they get help? I ^help them to get to safety. The passengers ^are grateful. I ^am proud that I remain calm.

Proofreader's Marks

Add text:
I ^show them what to do.

See all Proofreader's Marks on page ix.

Name ______________________ Date ______________

5 Write Complete Sentences

Remember: You need a **subject** and a **predicate** to make a complete sentence. Often, the most important word in the subject is a **noun**. Every predicate needs a **verb**.

Subject	Predicate
My older **brother**	always **teases** me.
His **friends**	**give** me a hard time, too.
My **sister**	usually **spends** time with me.
My whole **family**	**enjoys** each other most of the time.

Try It

A. Write a subject, a verb, or a predicate to complete each sentence. Possible responses:

1. My math homework is extremely hard tonight.
2. Usually, I finish my homework by myself.
3. Tonight, I need some help, though.
4. My older brother is very good at math.
5. He teases me all the time, though. I bet he won't help!

B. (6–10) Complete the subjects or predicates in this conversation between the two brothers. Possible responses:

James: Dan, my math is really hard. I don't get it.

Dan: Ah! My little brother needs help with his homework!

James: Forget it. It is not too hard for me.

Dan: Hey, James, I'm just kidding around. I understand that math. I'll help you.

James: Really? You'll help? So you are a pretty good big brother after all!

Write It

C. (11–14) Write your own conversation about another time when James asks Dan for help. Write one statement, one question, one exclamation, and one command. Remember to add the correct punctuation.

James: My ______________________ is ______________________

Dan: Do you ______________________

James: What a ______________________

Dan: Show me ______________________

D. (15–18) How do you and your siblings or friends get along? Write at least four sentences to explain. Use nouns in the subjects and verbs in the predicates.

____

____

____

____

____

Edit It

E. (19–25) Edit the journal entry. Fix the seven mistakes by adding missing nouns, verbs, and end punctuation. Possible responses:

February 26

Basketball is my favorite sport. My brother and sister never play with me, though[.] How surprised I am by this[!] I [am] outside shooting baskets. My big [brother] comes outside. He actually [plays] with me! Can you believe it[?] I guess I'm pretty lucky to have Dan for a big brother after all[!]

Proofreader's Marks

Add text:
I am surprised.

Add a period:
We play basketball.

Add a question mark:
Will you help me?

Add an exclamation point:
How shocked I am!

See all Proofreader's Marks on page ix.

Name ______________________ Date ____________

6 What's a Plural Noun?

A Word That Names More Than One Thing

One	More Than One
A **singular noun** names one thing.	A **plural noun** names more than one thing.

Use these spelling rules for forming plural nouns.

1. To make most nouns plural, just add **-s**.
2. If the noun ends in **s**, **z**, **sh**, **ch**, or **x**, add **-es**.
3. If the noun ends in **y** after the consonant, change the **y** to **i** and add **-es**.
4. Some nouns have special plural forms.

One	More Than One
hope	**hopes**
dish	**dishes**
memory	**memories**
child	**children**
man	**men**
woman	**women**

Try It

A. (1–4) Read these nouns: **children**, **dream**, **family**, **wishes**. Which nouns are singular and which are plural? Put each noun in the correct column. Then add its other form. The first one is done for you.

Singular Nouns (one)		Plural Nouns (more than one)	
child	dreams	children	dreams
family	wish	families	wishes

B. (5–10) Write nouns from the chart to complete the paragraph. Possible responses:

My ___family___ lives in the same building as two other ___families___. All of the ___children___ are good friends. We share a lot of the same ___wishes/dreams___ and ___dreams/wishes___. One ___dream/wish___ we all have is to go to college. I hope it comes true for all of us.

Write It

C. **How can you get to know someone well? Circle the singular noun in each question you might ask someone. Then use its plural form to answer the question.**

11. What city do you like to visit? Cities I like to visit are ______________________.

12. What is your favorite movie? ______________________

13. What country would you like to visit? ______________________

14. Do you like the beach? ______________________

D. **(15–18) Write at least four sentences about people you know well. Use at least two singular nouns and two plural nouns in your response.**

____

____

____

____

____

Edit It

E. **(19–25) Edit the journal entry. Fix the seven mistakes with nouns.**

November 4

I thought I knew my mother really well. Then she surprised me. She told me many ~~story~~ stories about her youth. Mom had a lot of ~~hobby~~ hobbies. She had two ~~bicycle~~ bicycles. She used to cycle all over the city. Sometimes she went on ~~trip~~ trips to other ~~country~~ countries. One of her ~~wish~~ wishes was to cycle around the world. One of my ~~dream~~ dreams is to go with her.

Proofreader's Marks

Change text:

My parents were ~~childs~~ children once.

See all Proofreader's Marks on page ix.

Name ______________________________ Date ______________

7 How Do You Know What Verb to Use?

Match It to the Subject.

- Use **I** with **am**.
  I **am** a volunteer.
- Use **he**, **she**, or **it** with **is**.
  It **is** a good experience for me.
  My job **is** to read to a child.
  He **is** happy to see me.
- Use **we**, **you**, or **they** with **are**.
  My friends **are** volunteers, too.
  They **are** volunteers at the soup kitchen.
  We **are** happy to help out. **Are** you?

Forms of *Be*
I **am**
he, she, or it **is**
we, you, or they **are**

Try It

A. (1–6) Write am, is, or are to complete the paragraph.

I ____am____ a volunteer at the neighborhood community center. My friend Annie ____is____ a volunteer, too. She ____is____ quiet about her volunteer work, though. People ____are____ surprised when they learn that she is so involved. I ____am____ happy to share the time with her. It ____is____ good to feel that we are helping out.

B. (7–12) Write am, is, or are to complete the interview with Annie.

Reporter: What ____are____ your favorite activities?

Annie: Well, I ____am____ always busy. Soccer ____is____ my favorite sport.

Reporter: When ____are____ the practices for soccer?

Annie: They ____are____ every day after school. My volunteer work ____is____ rewarding, too.

Write It

C. Complete the sentences to tell about some of your extracurricular activities. Use **am**, **is**, or **are** in each sentence.

13. I ______________ busy because ______________________________________
____.

14. My favorite activity ____.

15. Extracurricular activities ______________ important because ______________
____.

D. (16–19) Write at least four sentences to tell how two of your friends spend their time after school. Use **am**, **is**, and **are**.

____
____
____
____
____

Edit It

E. (20–25) Edit the letter. Fix the six mistakes with verbs.

Dear Uncle Ted,

I am very busy these days. You would be surprised to find out how much I do after school. My theater group keeps me really busy. It ~~are~~ is my favorite activity. The play ~~are~~ is next weekend, so we ~~is~~ are in rehearsals every day.

I am also a volunteer at the community center. I have a part-time job, too. It ~~am~~ is only a few hours a week, but it helps me save money for college. How busy I ~~are~~ am these days!

Your favorite nephew,

Michael

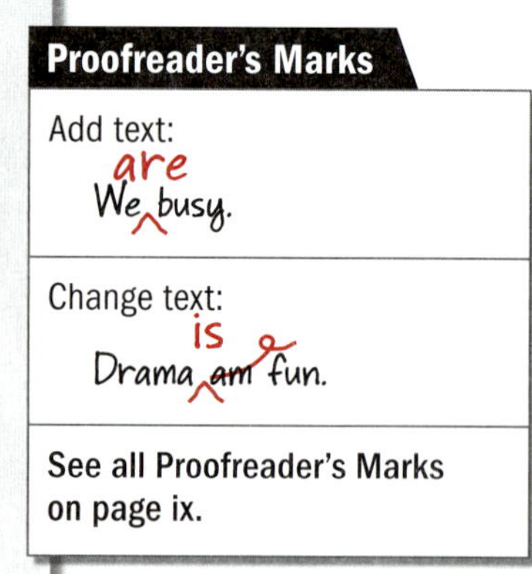

Name ______________________________ Date ______________

8 How Do You Know What Action Verb to Use?

Match It to the Subject.

- **Action verbs** tell when a subject does something, like **work**, **hike**, or **ride**. If the sentence is about one other person, place, or thing, add **-s** to the action verb.

1. My grandparents **work** hard.	**2.** Grandpa **works** at the hospital.
3. They **volunteer**, too.	**4.** Grandma **volunteers** at the library.
5. I **hike** with my grandmother.	**6.** She **hikes** in the mountains.

- If there is more than one action verb in a sentence, all verbs must agree with the subject:

  My grandparents **ride** bikes, **swim**, and **participate** in a book club.

Try It

A. Complete these sentences. Write the correct form of the verbs in parentheses.

1. The Lopezes ____act____ a lot younger than they are. **(act)**
2. Mrs. Lopez ____turns____ 80 this year. **(turn)**
3. She ____takes____ her dogs for a long walk every day. **(take)**
4. Sometimes, they even ____jog____ past my house! **(jog)**
5. I ____hope____ that I'm that active when I'm 80. **(hope)**

B. Write action verbs to complete these sentences. Make sure each verb agrees with the subject. Possible responses:

6. Mr. Lopez ____works____ in his garden.
7. His seeds ____blossom____ into beautiful flowers every year.
8. Sometimes, I ____help____ Mr. Lopez with the hard tasks.
9. Mr. Lopez ____teaches____ at the local college, too.
10. His students ____learn____ about plants from him.

Write It

C. Imagine that you are a volunteer at your local senior center. What activities do people do there? Complete the sentences. Use action verbs correctly.

11. That man ______________________________.

12. Those women ______________________________.

13. My grandfather ______________________________.

14. The people ______________, ______________, and ______________________________.

D. (15–18) Write at least four sentences to tell what your older relatives do to keep active. Use action verbs correctly.

____

____

____

____

____

Edit It

E. (19–25) Edit the article from *Senior News*. Fix the seven mistakes with action verbs.

Senior Citizens Plan Trip to the City

The Holyoke Senior Citizen Center is an active place. Members ~~comes~~ come every day to enjoy the activities. Some people take part in the daily bridge game. Other active seniors ~~plays~~ play in the tennis league. Mr. Lopez ~~organize~~ organizes trips to the city. Participating members ~~steps~~ step onto the bus. The bus ~~take~~ takes them to the city. The tourists ~~visits~~ visit museums and shop in the stores. Then they return home and ~~waits~~ wait for next month's trip.

Proofreader's Marks

Change text: People ~~rides~~ ride to the city.

See all Proofreader's Marks on page ix.

Name ______________________ Date ____________

9 What's a Compound Subject?

It's a Subject with Two or More Nouns.

When a subject has two or more nouns joined by **and** or **or**, it is called a **compound subject**.

1. **Trumpets and trombones** are brass instruments.
2. **Joyce and Carlos** play brass instruments in the band.
3. The **oboe or** the **flutes** play a solo.
4. The **clarinet or** the **piccolo** is my favorite instrument.

How do you know what verb to use with a compound subject?

- If you see **and**, use a plural verb like **are** or **play**.
- If you see **or**, look at the last noun in the subject.
  If it is singular, use a singular verb.
  If it is plural, use a plural verb.

Try It

A. Write the correct form of the verbs to complete the sentences.

1. Carlos and his band ___play___ (**play / plays**) really loud music.
2. Either the drums or the keyboard ___is___ (**is / are**) the loudest of all.
3. Mr. and Mrs. Green ___say___ (**say / says**) the music hurts their ears.
4. Each day, Mr. Green or Mrs. Suarez ___complains___ (**complain / complains**) about the noise.
5. Carlos and his friends ___want___ (**want / wants**) to do something nice for the neighbors.
6. Carlos and the drummer ___arrange___ (**arrange / arranges**) a free concert.
7. Kids and adults ___come___ (**come / comes**) to hear them.

B. Choose words from each column to build four sentences. You can use words more than once. Possible responses:

The drummer or the guitarist My neighbor or my parents The musician and his neighbors The band and my dad	complain dance agree plays	all day and all night. when the music plays. about putting on a free concert. about the loud music.

8. The drummer or the guitarist plays all day and all night.

9 My neighbor or my parents complain about the loud music.

10. The musician and his neighbors agree about putting on a free concert.

11. The band and my dad dance when the music plays.

Write It

C. Complete each sentence so that it tells about a band. Use the correct form of the verb.

12. My friends and I ______________________.

13. Your friends or your parents ______________________.

14. The keyboard and the bass ______________________.

15. The singer or the drummer ______________________.

D. (16–20) Imagine you are in a band. Write at least five sentences to tell about your band and what it might do for the community. Use a compound subject in each sentence. Use both **and** and **or**.

____

____

____

____

____

Name ________________ Date ________

10 Make Subjects and Verbs Agree

Remember: The verb you use depends on your subject. These subjects and verbs go together:

Forms of *Be*

I **am** strong.

You **are** strong.

He, she, or it **is** strong.

We, you, or they **are** strong.

My friends **are** strong.

My friends and I **are** strong.

Action Verbs

I **learn** about people's strengths.

You **learn** about people's strengths.

He, she, or it **learns** about people's strengths.

We, you, or they **learn** about people's strengths.

My friends **learn** about people's strengths.

My friends and I **learn** about people's strengths.

Try It

A. Complete each sentence. Write the correct form of the verb.

1. Sometimes, I ___decide___ to try something new. (decide / decides)
2. For example, my school ___holds___ baseball tryouts every year. (hold / holds)
3. The athletic director or the coach ___announces___ tryouts. (announce / announces)
4. Mom and Dad ___think___ I should try out. (think / thinks)
5. I ___am___ not sure that I'm good enough. (is / am)

B. (6–10) Write the correct form of a verb to complete each sentence. Possible responses:

I ___want___ to be on the team, though. Baseball ___is___ my favorite sport. My friends and my parents ___encourage___ me. My big brother ___helps___ me practice. The team list comes out. Hooray! I ___am___ on the team!

Write It

C. **Answer the questions about how you push your limits. Make sure your subjects and verbs agree.**

11. How do you push your limits? I ______________________________.

12. Who helps you? My ______________ and my ______________________.

13. What is one of your strengths? One strength ______________________.

14. What does that strength help you learn about yourself? It ______________________

____.

D. **(15–18) How have you surprised yourself by pushing your personal limits? Write at least four sentences. Use simple subjects and compound subjects. Make sure the subjects and verbs agree.**

____

____

____

____

Edit It

E. **(19–25) Edit the journal entry. Fix the seven mistakes in subject-verb agreement.**

July 12

Sometimes I really pull through for myself. My experiences ~~teaches~~ teach me to trust myself. If my mom ~~need~~ needs help, I ~~wants~~ want to be there for her. The same goes for my baseball team. The coach or the captain ~~give~~ gives me encouragement. We all ~~works~~ work together. They ~~is~~ are sometimes surprised by what I can accomplish. I ~~feels~~ feel the same way!

Proofreader's Marks

Change text:

We ~~knows~~ know ourselves and ~~pushes~~ push our limits.

See all Proofreader's Marks on page ix.

Name ______________________ Date ____________

11 What Is a Fragment?

It's an Incomplete Sentence.

A **fragment** is a group of words that begins with a capital letter and ends with a period. It looks like a sentence, but it is not complete. A subject or a verb may be missing.

Fragments	Sentences
1. Is a big city high school.	My school is a big city high school.
2. Has thousands of kids in it.	It has thousands of kids in it.
3. Many of the students.	Many of the students hang out together.
4. My friends members of one group.	My friends are members of one group.

Try It

A. Write whether each group of words is a fragment or a sentence. If it is a fragment, add a subject or a verb. Write the complete sentence. Possible responses:

1. Some groups of students athletes. fragment; Some groups of students are athletes.

2. Hang out together. fragment; The athletes hang out together.

3. Another group likes math, music, and computers. sentence

4. People that group is really smart. fragment; People think that group is really smart.

B. Fix the fragments. Add a subject or a verb. Possible responses:

5. My friends and I ^are friendly with all the groups.

6. ^We ~~P~~lay sports.

7. I ^compete on the math team, too.

8. All of the groups ^have interesting kids in them.

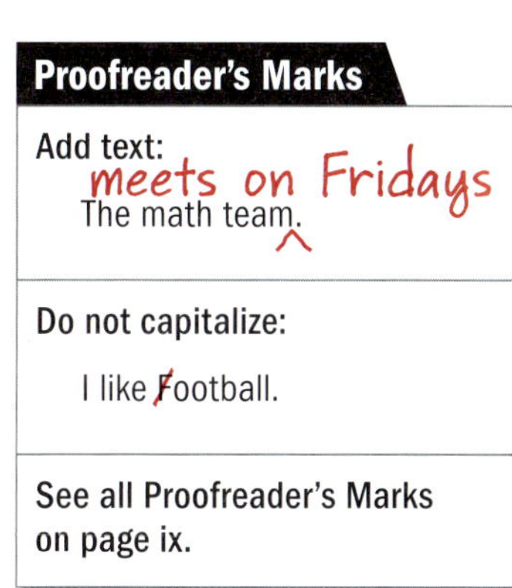
Proofreader's Marks

Add text: The math team ^meets on Fridays.

Do not capitalize: I like ~~F~~ootball.

See all Proofreader's Marks on page ix.

Write It

C. **Answer the questions about groups in your school. Use complete sentences.**

9. What groups exist in your high school? ____________________

____

10. What groups are you part of? ____________________

____

11. How do the groups get along with each other? ____________________

____

D. **(12–15) Write at least four sentences to tell what you think about different high school groups. Then read your sentences aloud. Fix any fragments that you might hear.**

____

____

____

____

____

Edit It

E. **(16–20) Edit the journal entry. Fix the five fragments.** Possible responses:

September 29

I am a new kid in this high school. At first, ^I was really worried. My old high school had a lot of groups. ^It ~~W~~was hard to make friends there. Everyone in this school ^gets along, though. All the kids ^are friendly. I have many new friends. Some of them ^play sports. Others are in the drama club. The kids are all nice to each other.

Proofreader's Marks

Add text:
Manny ^edits the student newspaper.

Do not capitalize:
I attend a ~~S~~school in the city.

See all Proofreader's Marks on page ix.

Name ______________________ Date __________

12 What's One Way to Fix a Fragment?

Add a Subject.

- A complete sentence has a **subject** and a **predicate**.
- To check for a subject, ask yourself: Whom or what is the sentence about?

Fragments	Sentences
1. Play sports.	**Athletes** play sports.
2. Have other interests, too.	**They** have other interests, too.
3. Plays football and writes for the student newspaper.	**Alex** plays football and writes for the student newspaper.

Try It

See all Proofreader's Marks on page ix.

A. **Fix each fragment. Add a subject to turn the fragment into a complete sentence.** Possible responses:

1. A musician plays a musical instrument. (Plays a musical instrument.)
2. An artist paints on a canvas. (Paints on a canvas.)
3. An athlete is really good at sports. (Is really good at sports.)
4. Many people are good at more than one thing. (Are good at more than one thing.)

B. **Write whether each group of words is a fragment or a sentence. If it is a fragment, add a subject to make a sentence about José, an athlete who doesn't fit into a stereotype. Write the complete sentence.** Possible responses:

5. Some people think athletes are only interested in sports. sentence
6. Is a really good athlete. fragment; My friend José is a really good athlete.
7. Plays saxophone in the jazz band, too. fragment; He plays saxophone in the jazz band, too.

Write It

C. **Answer the questions to tell your opinions about stereotypes. Use complete sentences.**

8. What is the stereotype of an athlete? An athlete ______________________________

____.

9. What do you think artists are like? I think artists ______________________________

____.

10. What do you think band members are like? I think band members ____________________

____.

11. Are stereotypes usually accurate? Explain. Stereotypes ___________________________

____.

D. (12–15) **Write at least four complete sentences about someone you know who doesn't fit a stereotype. Then read your sentences aloud. Fix any fragments.**

____

____

____

____

____

Edit It

E. (16–20) **Edit this letter. Fix the five fragments.** Possible responses:

Dear Bella,

I met a new friend today. ^John is a big football star. I don't like football players. ^Football players are only good at football. That's what I used to think, anyway. Now ^I know better. John is really good at math. ^He is on the math team with me. ^We get along together really well. I guess I learned a lesson about stereotypes!

Love,

Caitlin

Proofreader's Marks

Add text:
We ^are friends.

Do not capitalize:
We should not ~~S~~tereotype.

Name ________________ Date ________

13 What's Another Way to Fix a Fragment?

Add a Predicate, and Be Sure It Has a Verb.

When you write a sentence, be sure to include the verb. If you leave the verb out, the words you wrote are a **fragment**. Study the sentences in the chart.

Fragments	Sentences
1. I this information in the newspaper.	I **read** this information in the newspaper.
2. Firstborn children higher IQs than their siblings.	Firstborn children **have** higher IQs than their siblings.
3. All the children in my family smart!	All the children in my family **are** smart!

Try It

A. Fix each fragment. Add a verb to turn the fragment into a complete sentence.

Possible responses:

1. Some people ^think that youngest siblings are spoiled.
2. That belief ^is one kind of stereotype.
3. That stereotype ^makes no sense to me.
4. My youngest sibling ^acts the same as the rest of us.

B. Write whether each group of words is a **fragment** or a **sentence**. If it is a fragment, add a verb to write a sentence about family stereotypes. Possible responses:

5. Marianna my youngest sister. fragment; Marianna is my youngest sister.
6. Some youngest siblings spoiled. fragment; Some youngest siblings are spoiled.
7. Marianna does all her chores. sentence
8. My parents Marianna and me the same. fragment; My parents treat Marianna and me the same.

Write It

C. Fix the fragments by adding predicates. Write sentences about family stereotypes.

9. Family stereotypes. ______________________________

10. The oldest child. ______________________________

11. The middle children. ______________________________

12. Working moms. ______________________________

D. (13–15) Write at least three sentences about stereotypes and your family. Then read your sentences aloud. Fix any fragments you might hear.

____

____

____

____

____

Edit It

E. (16–20) Edit this student's report about family stereotypes. Fix the five fragments.

Possible responses:

Family Stereotypes

Some people think that dads don't help around the house. I think that is a stereotype. My dad ^helps around our house all the time. Every morning, he ^makes breakfast for me. On the weekends, he ^mows the lawn. Sometimes he ^cooks dinner, too. My dad ^watches a lot of baseball on TV, too. Every family is different. I've learned not to believe in stereotypes.

Proofreader's Marks

Add text: My dad ^is a great guy.

See all Proofreader's Marks on page ix.

Name ______________________ Date ______________

14 What's One More Way to Fix a Fragment?

Combine Neighboring Sentences.

Writers may create a fragment by starting a new sentence when they shouldn't. These fragments are easy to fix. Just combine the fragment with the sentence before it.

1. I live in a neighborhood. (sentence) That is multicultural. (fragment)
   I live in a neighborhood that is multicultural.

2. I enjoy my neighborhood. (sentence) Because I learn a lot about different cultures. (fragment)
   I enjoy my neighborhood because I learn a lot about different cultures.

Try It

A. Combine each fragment with the neighboring sentence. Write the new sentence.

1. My parents moved to our neighborhood from Italy. When I was a baby. My parents moved to our neighborhood from Italy when I was a baby.

2. My neighbors moved here from Greece. Before I started school. My neighbors moved here from Greece before I started school.

3. We are close friends. Even though we have different backgrounds. We are close friends even though we have different backgrounds.

4. We have many neighbors. Who come from countries all around the world. We have many neighbors who come from countries all around the world.

5. Every summer, the whole neighborhood gets together. And has a huge potluck dinner.
   Every summer, the whole neighborhood gets together and has a huge potluck dinner.

6. I love those dinners. Because I get to taste food from all around the world. I love those dinners because I get to taste food from all around the world.

B. Combine the fragments with the sentences to make new sentences. You can use sentences and fragments more than once. Possible responses:

Sentences	Fragments
I do not pay attention to stereotypes.	And consider this neighborhood our home.
My neighbors come from different backgrounds.	Because I live in a multicultural neighborhood.
My neighbors and I live next to each other.	But are still my friends.

7. I do not pay attention to stereotypes because I live in a multicultural neighborhood.

8. My neighbors come from different backgrounds but are still my friends.

9. My neighbors and I live next to each other and consider this neighborhood our home.

Write It

C. Fix each fragment about stereotypes by combining it with a sentence. Write your new sentences.

10. Because the students come from many countries. ______________________

11. Even though my best friend is from India. ______________________

12. Before I tasted Chinese food. ______________________

D. (13–15) Would you like to live in a multicultural neighborhood? Write at least three sentences to explain your reasons. Read your sentences aloud. Fix any fragments.

____

Name ______________________ Date ____________

15 Fix Sentence Fragments

Remember: You can fix a fragment by adding a subject or a predicate that includes a verb. Or, you can combine the fragment with another sentence.

Fragment: Takes time to make a new friend.
Sentence: It takes time to make a new friend.

Fragment: People their thoughts and feelings.
Sentence: People share their thoughts and feelings.

Fragment: Friends don't make assumptions. Before they know each other.
Sentence: Friends don't make assumptions before they know each other.

Try It

A. Fix the fragments. Write the new sentences.

1. Ava always purple socks. Ava always wears purple socks.
2. I think she is weird. Because of her appearance. I think she is weird because of her appearance.
3. Then bump into Ava at the basketball court. Then I bump into Ava at the basketball court.
4. She is a fantastic athlete. And is really funny, too. She is a fantastic athlete and is really funny, too.

B. Change each fragment into a sentence about getting to know Ava. Write your sentences.

Possible responses:

5. Ava and I. Ava and I become friends.
6. Learn not to make assumptions about people. I learn not to make assumptions about people.
7. Because Ava is a lot like me. I'm lucky I get to know Ava because Ava is a lot like me.

Write It

C. Answer the questions about getting to know people. Make sure you use complete sentences.

8. Why is it important to get to know people? It is important to get to know people because ______________________________ ______________________________.

9. Why shouldn't you make assumptions before you know someone? Assumptions ______________ ______________________________.

10. What is the best way to get to know someone? The best way to get to know someone is ______________________________ ______________________________.

D. (11–15) Write at least five sentences about getting to know a new friend. Then read your sentences aloud. Fix any fragments.

____

____

____

____

____

Edit It

E. (16–20) Edit the paragraph. Fix the five fragments. Possible responses:

All around the world, people are different from one another. We shouldn't make judgments about those people. Until we meet them. It [takes] time to get to know new people. We can share our experiences. And our feelings with new acquaintances. Then [they] get to know us. We get to know them, too. In this way, we [look] beyond the stereotypes.

Proofreader's Marks

Delete:
I made a new friend. today.

Add text:
Her name [is] Jen.

Do not capitalize:
We are in Band together.

See all Proofreader's Marks on page ix.

Name ______________________ Date ______________

Capitalize Proper Nouns and Adjectives

- **Proper nouns** are capitalized because they name specific people, places, and things. Common nouns, which are general, are not capitalized.

Common Noun	Proper Noun
teacher	Mrs. Carson
city	Chicago

- **Proper adjectives**, which come from proper nouns, are also capitalized.

Proper Noun	Proper Adjective
Chicago	Chicagoan
Italy	Italian

Try It

Proofreader's Marks

Capitalize:

He is from chicago.

Do not capitalize:

He likes Italian Music.

See all Proofreader's Marks on page ix.

A. Use proofreader's marks to correct the capitalization errors in each sentence.

1. When I was in third grade, my teacher, mrs. riggs, taught me how to play the piano.
2. My favorite piece to play was written by a german Composer.
3. By the time I was in sixth grade, I had also learned how to play the spanish guitar.
4. Later that year, I decided to go to the State music competition in detroit.
5. I placed second in the Piano Competition. Afterwards, dad took me to my favorite restaurant to celebrate.
6. After sixth grade, my family and I moved to los angeles.
7. In my Freshman Year, I joined the high school orchestra.
8. I discovered the Music of Aaron Copland. Now I want to be a Composer.

Name ______________________ Date ______________

Use Serial Commas Correctly

Serial commas are used to separate three or more words, phrases, or clauses written in a series. There should be a comma after each item in the series except the last one.

1. Rosa plays soccer, tennis, **and** basketball.
2. She ran down the field, kicked the ball, **and** scored the winning goal.
3. After the game, do you want to get pizza, hamburgers, **or** tacos?

Try It

A. (9–15) Edit the story. Fix the seven punctuation mistakes.

I have always loved music. My mom said that when I was just three years old, I used to bang on pots, pans, and tabletops as if they were drums. As soon as Dad put on the radio, I started humming the tune, drumming rhythms, and dancing along with the music.

Now that I am in high school, I play in the school orchestra. I can play the piano, cello, and drums. My dad is teaching me how to play the guitar. I'm going to play the guitar, piano, cello, and drums at our next school concert. I'm nervous, excited, and scared, but with Mom and Dad cheering me on, I think I will do just fine.

Proofreader's Marks

Add a comma:

Today, we will study science, history, French, and math.

Delete:

I teach piano, guitar, and drums, to younger students.

B. Put the words in the right order. Write the sentence using the correct punctuation.

16. spend time volunteering / I play basketball / and practice piano / every week

I play basketball, spend time volunteering, and practice piano every week.

17. are Beethoven / some of / Mozart and Copland / my favorite composers

Some of my favorite composers are Beethoven, Mozart, and Copland.

Name ______________________________ Date ______________

Edit and Proofread

✓ Check Your Spelling

Homonyms are words that sound alike but have different meanings and spellings. Spell these homonyms correctly when you proofread.

Homonyms and Their Meanings	Examples
it's (contraction) = it is; it has	**It's** fun to learn a new song.
its (adjective) = belonging to it	I play cello. I like **its** sound.
there (adverb) = that place or position	My first year **there** I joined the choir.
their (adjective) = belonging to them	**Their** music program is the best.
they're (contraction) = they are	**They're** going to the state music competition.

Try It

Proofreader's Marks

Change text: They practice ~~they're~~ their skills.

A. **Use proofreader's marks to correct the spelling errors in the following sentences.**

18. Our school is having a talent show next month. ~~Its~~ It's sponsored by the student council.

19. ~~Their~~ They're signing up anyone who wants to be in the show.

20. ~~It's~~ Its goal is to raise money for a local family who lost ~~there~~ their home in a fire.

21. ~~They're~~ There are a lot of talented students in our school.

B. **(22–27) Write a short paragraph about an event at your school. Use at least six homonyms in your paragraph.**

____

____

____

____

____

____

____

Name ______________________ Date ____________

Fix Run-on Sentences

A **run-on sentence** consists of two or more sentences written incorrectly as one sentence.

- To fix a run-on sentence, break it into shorter sentences. Replace the comma with end punctuation. Then start the second sentence with a capital letter.

  Incorrect: I want to learn how to play the cello, **since** I already know how to play the guitar, it should be easy to learn the cello.

  Correct: I want to learn how to play the cello. **Since** I already know how to play the guitar, it should be easy to learn the cello.

- Sometimes you can fix a run-on sentence by replacing the comma with a semicolon.

  Incorrect: I wanted to play guitar, **I** like its sound.

  Correct: I wanted to play guitar; **I** like its sound.

Try It

A. Read each sentence and write if it is a run-on or not. Fix each run-on and write the new sentence.

28. One day my dad offered to give me guitar lessons, from then on, we practiced together every evening. run-on sentence; One day my dad offered to give me guitar lessons. From then on, we practiced together every evening.

29. That same year, my teacher, Mrs. Carson, volunteered to give me piano lessons after school. not a run-on sentence

30. Since I could already play guitar, I thought I would not have to practice much at piano, at first, I learned quickly. run-on sentence; Since I could already play guitar, I thought I would not have to practice much at piano. At first, I learned quickly.

Name ________________________ Date ____________

16 Is the Subject of a Sentence Always a Noun?

No, It Can Be a Pronoun.

- Use **I** when you talk about yourself.
  I saw the sign from the bus window.
- Use **you** when you talk to another person.
  Are **you** interested in volunteering?
- Use **he** when you talk about one man or one boy.
  Use **she** when you talk about one woman or one girl.
  Sorija Ramirez is a doctor.
  She tells me to come back on Tuesday.
- Use **it** when you talk about one place, thing, or idea.
  The program is starting soon. **It** will be interesting.

Subject Pronouns
Singular
I
you
he, she, it

Try It

A. Complete each sentence about someone who discovers a new interest. Use the subject pronouns I, you, he, she, or it.

1. Dr. Ramirez told me about her program. ___She___ told me how I could help.
2. She said to me, "___You___ would be a great volunteer."
3. I am excited. ___I___ will help the patients and doctors.
4. Medicine is a good career. ___It___ is interesting.

B. (5–8) **Write the correct pronoun to complete the sentence.**

My dad didn't know I was volunteering. ___He___ asked about this new interest. Dr. Ramirez told me about her education. ___She___ explained how much school she completed. I thought about my classes this year so far. ___I___ will need to improve my grades. Dr. Ramirez told me she wasn't always the best student. ___She___ worked very hard to become a doctor.

Write It

C. Answer the questions about a new interest. Use subject pronouns.

9. In the past year, what new interest or hobby have you discovered? In the past year, ____________ have discovered ____________________.

10. How did you discover this interest? ____________________

____

11. Who was surprised by your new interest? Why? ____________________

____

D. (12–15) Write at least four sentences that tell more about your new interest or hobby. Use subject pronouns.

____

____

____

____

____

Edit It

E. (16–20) Edit the letter. Fix the five mistakes in subject pronouns.

Dear Marissa,

Today I started volunteering at the hospital. ~~He~~ I love it! Dr. Ramirez introduced me to the patients. ~~I~~ She is well liked by everyone. ~~Me~~ You would like her, too. Mr. Raul is one of the patients. ~~She~~ He is a kind man. I like helping people. I want to be a doctor. I will need to study hard in school.

Your friend,

Ella

Proofreader's Marks

Change text:
~~He~~ She is helpful.

Add text:
She told me what to study.

See all Proofreader's Marks on page ix.

Name ______________________________ Date ______________

17 Can a Pronoun Show "More Than One"?

Yes, It Can.

- Use **we** to talk about yourself and another person.

  Omar and I talked about our writing.

  We talked about my story.

- Use **you** to talk to one or more persons.

  You are talented, Omar.

  You are all talented writers.

- Use **they** to talk about more than one person or thing.

  The students listened to my story. **They** laughed and clapped.

Subject Pronouns	
Singular	**Plural**
I	we
you	you
he, she, it	they

Try It

A. Read the first sentence. Complete the second sentence with we, you, or they.

1. Ms. Stone leads our writing club. ____We____ meet every Wednesday.
2. When she read our work, she said, "____You____ are all very good writers."
3. We write one story a month. ____We____ sometimes read our work aloud.
4. The students listened to my story. ____They____ liked it a lot.
5. After the meeting, Ms. Stone talked to us. She said, "____You____ should publish your stories."
6. We talked about magazines that might publish our stories. ____We____ made a plan to send them to the magazines.
7. The other students are excited. ____They____ want to be published.

B. Choose words from each column to write five sentences. You may use words more than once.

We You They	give suggest should think choose	the magazine will buy it. publish your stories. ways to improve it. the magazines we like to read. me confidence.

Possible responses:

8. The students give comments about each story. They suggest ways to improve it.

9. We look at magazines together. We choose the magazines we like to read.

10. Ms. Stone says to us, "You should take a chance." You should publish your stories.

11. All of the students encourage me. They give me confidence.

12. My teacher and I decide to send the story to a magazine. We think the magazine will buy it.

Write It

C. Answer the questions about a group that takes a chance, based on their abilities. Use **we**, **you**, or **they**.

13. What sports team or other group do you know that took a chance and succeeded?

_______________ *succeeded because* _______________.

14. How did this group take a chance? _______________

15. Who was a critic of this group? _______________ *criticized them, but* _______________.

D. (16–20) Write at least five sentences that tell more about when this group took a chance. Use plural subject pronouns.

____

____

____

____

____

Name ______________________ Date ____________

18 Can a Compound Subject Include a Pronoun?

Yes, and the Pronoun Comes Last.

A **compound subject** can include nouns and pronouns joined by **and** or **or**.

1. My **teammates and I** will win this year.
2. **Parents and students** think the competition is tough.
3. The **team and I** are excited.
4. The **coach or the captain** has to help us.
5. **Tracy, Janine, or I** have to lead the team.

How do you know where to place the pronoun?

- Nouns always come before pronouns.
- The pronoun **I** always comes last.

Try It

A. Complete each sentence. Write the correct compound subject.

1. Our coach and I think we have a small team.
   Our coach and I / I and our coach

2. Sandra and Ms. Smith work on speed. Ms. Smith and she think that speed is our best skill.
   Ms. Smith and she / She and Ms. Smith

3. The two teachers and we gather extra equipment.
   The two teachers and we / We and the two teachers

4. Chris, the captain, and I know there are few resources for us.
   Chris, the captain, and I / The captain, I, and Chris

5. Sarah, Sandra, and I save a little money each week.
   Sarah, Sandra, and I / I, Sarah, and Sandra

6. Ms. Smith, the captain, and I think having heart is more important than resources.
   the captain, and I / I, and the captain

B. **Rewrite each sentence. Fix the compound subjects.**

7. My mom, I, sister, and brother patch up the uniforms.
My mom, sister, brother, and I patch up the uniforms.

8. Our neighbors, we, and friends think we have a lot of potential.
Our neighbors, friends, and we think we have a lot of potential.

9. But they or the opposing school often think we won't win.
But the opposing school or they often think we won't win.

10. She, I, or he will help with new plays.
She, he, or I will help with new plays.

11. We and the top two players have several strategies.
The top two players and we have several strategies.

12. They, I, and Chris like to surprise the other team.
Chris, they, and I like to surprise the other team.

Write It

C. **Answer the questions about a team or an organization that exceeded expectations. Use compound subjects.**

13. How does an underdog team win? The players aren't expected to win. ______
______ play with less pressure.

14. How do members of the team overcome challenges? ______

15. Who thought the team would fail? ______

D. **(16–20) Write at least five sentences that tell more about the team or organization that exceeded expectations. Use compound subjects.**

______

______

______

______

______

Name ______________________ Date ______________

19 How Do You Avoid Confusion with Pronouns?

Match the Pronoun to the Noun.

If you're not sure which **pronoun** to use, first find the **noun** it goes with. Then ask yourself:

- Is the noun a man or a woman?
  Use **he** for a man and **she** for a woman.
- Is the noun singular or plural? If plural, use **they**.

If a pronoun does not refer correctly to a noun, change the pronoun.

Incorrect: **Jesse** waits for the response. **It** feels nervous.

Correct: **Jesse** waits for the response. **He** feels nervous.

The pronouns in these sentences are correct. Do you know why?

1. **Teachers** think Jesse is irresponsible. **They** remember him in class.
2. **Jesse** makes changes. **He** also writes an essay about his goals.

Try It

A. Read the first sentence. Complete the second sentence with the correct pronoun.

1. Jesse wants to run for class president. ___He___ is taking it very seriously.
2. The teachers are not confident about Jesse's ability. ___They___ think he doesn't work hard in class.
3. Ms. Browne wants to give Jesse another chance. ___She___ asks him to write an essay to describe his goals.
4. Ms. Browne and the other teachers will read the essay. ___They___ will read it next week.
5. Mr. Shepard is the first teacher to read it. ___He___ thinks Jesse has a lot of talent.
6. The essay includes five goals. ___It___ describes Jesse's leadership.

B. **Draw lines to logically connect the words in the first column with those in the second column.**

7. All of the teachers have read the essay, and — they like it.
8. Ms. Browne and Mr. Santoro found a tutor for Jesse. — They want to help him.
9. Mr. Shepard talked to the other teachers. — He wants Jesse to succeed.
10. Mara will tutor him. — She will meet with him on Tuesdays.

Write It

C. **Answer the questions about someone who exceeded expectations. Make sure the pronouns refer correctly to their nouns.**

11. Who do you know who changed to meet a goal? ______________________________

12. What did this person do to meet the goal? He/She ______________________________.

13. Who were the critics, and what did they say? ______________________________

D. **(14–16) Write at least three sentences that tell more about someone who exceeded expectations. Make sure pronouns refer correctly to nouns.**

____

____

____

Edit It

E. **(17–20) Edit the campaign flyer. Fix the four mistakes in pronouns.**

Vote for Jesse. He is a winner!

Students believe ~~it~~ he is a good leader. They believe in him! Our school needs change. ~~They~~ It can be better! Jesse will work for you. ~~It~~ He can work for improvements.

Proofreader's Marks

Add text: They will vote for him.

Change text: ~~He~~ She supports his election.

See all Proofreader's Marks on page ix.

Name ______________________________ Date ____________

20 Use Subject Pronouns

Remember: The subject of a sentence can be a pronoun. A **subject pronoun** can be singular or plural.

- Use **I** when you talk about yourself.
- Use **you** to talk to one or more persons.
- Use **we** to talk about another person and yourself.
- Use **he**, **she**, **it**, and **they** to talk about other people or things.

How do you know which pronoun to use? Look at the noun it goes with.

1. If the noun is a man or boy, use **he**. If it is a woman or girl, use **she**.
2. If the noun is a place or thing, use **it**. If the noun is plural, use **they**.

Try It

A. Complete each sentence with the correct subject pronoun.

1. Marisol leads the fundraising effort. ____She____ (They / She) thinks we can do it.
2. Our goal is to raise money for sports equipment. ____We____ (We / They) think we can sell food items.
3. Mr. Banderas will set up our booth. ____He____ (He / It) will let us sell baked goods.
4. The other coaches think raising money is too difficult. ____They____ (We / They) say equipment is too expensive.

B. Complete each sentence with the correct pronoun from the box.

he	it	she	they

5. All of the teams need equipment. ____They____ need helmets.
6. Jeff leads the Saturday car wash fundraiser. ____He____ raises a lot of money.
7. Victoria helps at the booth. ____She____ sells food to customers.
8. The fundraiser is a success. ____It____ attracts many people to the school.

Write It

C. **Answer the questions about a successful contest, competition, or fundraiser. Use subject pronouns.**

9. What did this group accomplish? ____________________

10. Who organized the effort, and how? ____________________

11. What made this team or group unusual? ____________________

____

12. What was the most memorable part of this group's or team's story? ____________________

____

D. (13–16) **Write at least four sentences about a group whose efforts were more successful than expected. Use subject pronouns correctly.**

____

____

____

____

____

Edit It

E. (17–20) **Edit the letter. Fix the four mistakes in subject pronouns.**

Dear Marisol:

You and your team did a great job. The school has money for equipment for next year. ~~They~~ It can buy helmets and other equipment. Mr. Banderas, Ms. Smith, and I are amazed at your efforts. ~~They~~ We think you did a great job. The teams are very happy. They can play safely and well next year. ~~He~~ I am very proud of you.

Sincerely,

Principal Johnson

Proofreader's Marks

Change text:
~~It~~ He liked the fundraiser.

Add text:
She sold pizzas.

See all Proofreader's Marks on page ix.

Name ______________________________ Date ______________

21 What Adds Action to a Sentence?

An Action Verb

- An **action verb** tells what the subject does. Some action verbs tell about an action that you cannot see.

  Minh **hikes** with his family.

  His father **likes** the mountains.

- Make sure the action verb agrees with its subject. Add **-s** if the subject tells about one place, one thing, or one other person.

  Minh buys a new pair of hiking boots.

  His **family camps** at the base of the mountain.

  He looks at the trail map.

  At night, **they plan** the climb to the top.

Try It

A. Write an action verb to complete each sentence. Possible responses:

1. Minh ____packs____ his gear in his backpack.
2. Minh and his parents ____cross____ a river in the morning.
3. Minh ____drinks____ a lot of water on the hike.

B. Complete each sentence about the hiking challenge. Write the correct action verb.

4. Minh's parents ____check____ Minh's gear.
   check / checks
5. Minh ____needs____ to be careful on this steep climb.
   need / needs
6. He ____climbs____ up the mountain.
   climb / climbs
7. Minh ____avoids____ looking down.
   avoid / avoids
8. Minh and his parents ____celebrate____ when they reach the top.
   celebrate / celebrates

Write It

C. **You are going on a camping trip with your friend's family. You have never hiked in the mountains before. How do you meet this challenge? Use action verbs.**

9. What do you do to prepare for the trip? I ______________________.

10. How do you make it over the rough terrain? I ______________________.

11. How do other people on the trip guide you? ______________________

____

12. What does your group do when you reach the summit? We ______________________

______________________.

D. **(13–15) Write at least three sentences about your success with a great challenge. Use action verbs.**

____

____

____

____

Edit It

E. **(16–20) Edit the postcard. Fix the five mistakes in verbs.**

Dear Mom and Dad,

We are on our way to base camp. Sarah pack^s the food. Her dad organize^s the tents. We helps plan the trip by using maps. I like the mountains. They are so beautiful. The sun shine^s brightly as we hike. I need to drink a lot of water here. On Wednesday, we makes the summit.

Love,

Brisa

Proofreader's Marks

Add text:

This hike challenge^s me.

Delete:

I stops to drink water.

See all Proofreader's Marks on page ix.

Name ______________________ Date __________

22 How Do You Know When the Action Happens?

Look at the Verb.

An **action verb** tells what the subject does. The tense of a verb tells when the action happens.

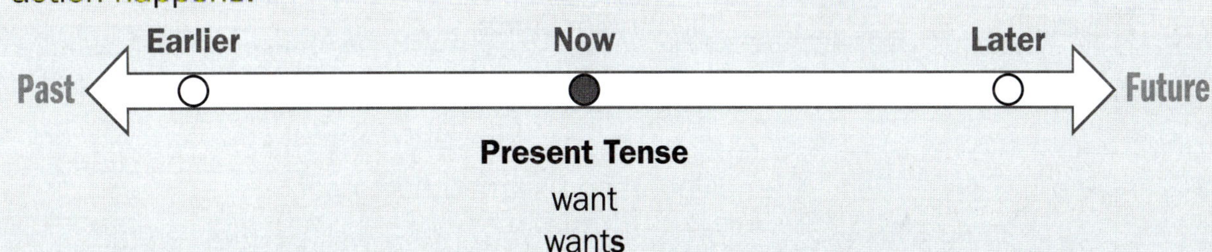

Present Tense

want

wants

Use the **present tense** to talk about actions that happen now or that happen on a regular basis.

Mr. Taylor **wants** a safe neighborhood.

Alvaro **helps** the citizens.

They **meet** with their neighbors every Monday.

Try It

A. Underline the verb in the first sentence. Rewrite the sentence, using a different verb. Possible responses:

1. Alvaro speaks to the teenagers in the neighborhood. Alvaro talks to the teenagers in the neighborhood.
2. They prevent crime in the area. They stop crime in the area.
3. Some people provide ideas for change. Some people give ideas for change.
4. The citizens notice less crime in the area. The citizens report less crime in the area.
5. Alvaro explains how proud he is of the teenagers. Alvaro says how proud he is of the teenagers.
6. Every day the teenagers gain something new from Alvaro. Every day the teenagers learn something new from Alvaro.

B. **Complete each sentence with a verb from the box. Use the correct form of the action verb.**

ask	buy	install	pick up	plant	receive	visit	work

7. The teens pick up garbage from the park.

8. The adults ask the city for lights.

9. Mr. Taylor buys lights with the funds.

10. Alvaro installs a neighborhood sign at the corner.

11. A group of gardeners plant flowers.

12. The neighbors work together to improve the area.

13. City leaders visit the neighborhood.

14. The neighbors receive an award for their improvements.

Write It

C. **Citizens in your neighborhood want your help to improve the area. You know how to build, plant, and complete home improvement projects. How do you offer to help your neighborhood? Use present tense action verbs.**

15. What do you do to help your neighborhood? I ______________________________.

16. How do people in your neighborhood work together? They ______________________________

______________________________.

17. Describe one way you work to improve your home or neighborhood. ______________________________

____

D. **(18–20) Write at least three sentences about ways that people improve their neighborhoods. Use present tense action verbs.**

____

____

____

____

Name ____________________ Date ____________

23 Which Action Verbs End in -s?

The Ones That Go with *He*, *She*, or *It*

- An **action verb** in the **present tense** tells about something that happens now or on a regular basis.
- Add **-s** to the action verb if the subject tells about one place, one thing, or one other person.

  Yuri **likes** science. He **works** hard in school.
- If the verb ends in **sh**, **ch**, **ss**, **s**, **x**, or **z**, add **-es**.

  Time **passes**. He **reaches** for a new challenge.
- Do not add **-s** to the action verb if the subject is **I**, **you**, **we**, **they**, or a plural noun.

  They **need** help at the zoo. You **call** Yuri. You **tell** him about a volunteer job.

Try It

A. Write the correct present tense verb to complete each sentence.

1. Yuri ___hopes___ to become a veterinarian. (hope / hopes)
2. The local college ___teaches___ classes to become a veterinarian. (teach / teaches)
3. Yuri's parents ___save___ money for college. (save / saves)
4. The college ___offers___ a scholarship. (offer / offers)

B. Write the correct present tense form of the verb in parentheses.

5. Yuri ___watches___ the animals at the zoo. **(watch)**
6. He ___learns___ about how to behave around large animals. **(learn)**
7. His family ___pushes___ him to succeed. **(push)**
8. They ___think___ he can get the scholarship. **(think)**

Write It

C. Answer the questions about your career goals. Use present tense verbs.

9. What profession or career are you interested in? I ______________________________

____.

10. What do you need to study for this career? To be a ______________, you ______________

____.

11. What can you do now to get ready for this career? ______________________________

____

12. How do your family members or teachers help you reach this goal? ______________

____

D. (13–15) **Write at least three sentences about what you can do to reach your career goal. Use present tense verbs.**

____

____

____

____

Edit It

E. (16–20) **Edit the letter. Fix the five mistakes in verbs.**

Dear Zoo Director:

I read your ad for volunteers. I think I can do this work. Our dog ^messes up our yard. I cleans it up, and I cares for four large dogs in our neighborhood. This work disgust^s my friends. I don't mind. I am good with animals. You gives great care to the zoo animals. I want to help.

Sincerely,

David Brennar

Proofreader's Marks

Add text:

Mr. ~~Brennar~~ Haas call^s me for the job.

Delete:

I start~~s~~ on Tuesday.

See all Proofreader's Marks on page ix.

Name ______________________ Date ____________

24 What Kinds of Verbs Are *Can*, *Could*, *May*, and *Might*?

They Are Helping Verbs.

- An action verb can have two parts: a **helping verb** and a **main verb**. The main verb shows the action.

  Today, Charles **walks** with a guide dog. He **may** **walk** into the city.

- Some helping verbs change the meaning of the action verb.

  1. Use **can** or **could** to tell about an ability.

  Charles **can** **walk** to many places.
  He **could** **walk** around in his building last month.

  2. Use **may**, **might**, or **could** to tell about a possibility.

  Charles **may** **walk** to the store. He **might** **visit** the museum, too.
  Charles **could** **walk** to the park if he has time.

- **Can**, **could**, **may**, and **might** stay the same with all subjects. Do not add **-s**.

  His dog **knows** what to do. She **can** **sense** danger. Charles **might** **enjoy** many new things with his guide dog.

Try It

A. Complete each sentence with **can**, **could**, **may**, or **might**. More than one answer is possible. Possible responses:

1. Charles always thought he ___could___ take care of a guide dog.

2. With the guide dog, he believes he ___can___ do anything.

3. Yesterday, they walked one-half mile. Tomorrow, they ___may or might___ walk a mile.

4. Charles ___may or might___ let the dog rest this afternoon.

5. His dog's name is Sally. She ___can___ help Charles get around the city.

6. Tomorrow, they ___may or might___ go to the beach.

B. **Complete each sentence with the appropriate helping verb.** Possible responses:

7. Sally is a Labrador retriever. She can (can / might) help Charles cross streets.

8. Charles takes care of her. He may (could / may) brush her on Tuesday.

9. Sally might (could / might) change Charles's life.

10. Sally knows how to help Charles on the bus. She can (can / might) help him board the bus.

11. Sally makes decisions near stairways. She may (could / may) stop Charles at the bottom of stairs.

12. Charles is responsible for giving commands. He can (can / could) tell Sally where to go.

13. Sally makes other decisions. She may (can / may) decide to stop without a command.

Write It

C. **Answer the questions about a pet as a companion. Use the helping verbs can, could, may, or might.**

14. Have you ever had a pet or known a friend's pet? What can pets do? A pet ____________________.

15. What might a dog do to comfort you? ____________________

16. What could you teach a pet to do? ____________________

D. **(17–20) Write at least four sentences about a pet you have or a friend has. Use can, could, may, and might.**

____

____

____

____

Name ______________________ Date ____________

25 Use Action Verbs in the Present Tense

Remember: A verb must agree with its subject.

- Subjects **I**, **you**, **we**, **they**, or **plural nouns** do not add **-s** on the **action verb**. Subjects that tell about one place, one thing, or one other person take **-s**.

I **dream** about a goal.	Natalya **dreams** about the Olympics.
You **believe** in her goals.	She **believes** she can win a medal.
We **motivate** each other.	The competition **motivates** people.
They **ask** how they can help.	Jared **asks** Natalya about her goals.

- These verbs don't change. Do you know why?

A coach **may help** Natalya.	She **might learn** new strategies.
He **can inspire** her to win.	She **could become** a medalist.

Try It

A. Choose the correct present tense verb to complete each sentence.

1. Natalya ___dreams___ about winning a medal. (dream / dreams)
2. Jared dreams that he ___may play___ in the major league. (may play / may plays)
3. They ___work___ to be the best. (work / works)
4. Their goals ___may lead___ to success. (may lead / mays lead)

B. Write the correct present tense form of the verb in parentheses.

5. Natalya ___wants___ to train every day. **(want)**
6. Her injury ___causes___ disappointment. **(cause)**
7. She ___trains___ again. **(train)**
8. Natalya ___learns___ the results of hard work. **(learn)**
9. Her medals ___hang___ in her room. **(hang)**

Write It

C. **Answer the questions about someone who doesn't give up on a dream. Use the correct form of present tense verbs.**

10. Who do you know who doesn't give up, even after failure? I ______________________________.

11. What can this person do that is special? This person ______________________________.

12. What might this person do in the future? ______________________________

D. **(13–15) Write at least three sentences about someone who overcame failure and became a success. Use some present tense verbs in your response.**

____

____

____

____

____

Edit It

E. **(16–20) Edit the postcard. Fix the five mistakes in present tense verbs.**

Dear Natalya,

Tomorrow is the big tennis tournament! I look forward to watching you compete.

My family like^s to watch you, too. They can comes with me. We are not sure, but ^may we ^bring the video camera. Your dream inspire^s me. We knows you can make it to the Olympics!

Love,

Katie

Proofreader's Marks

Delete:

I likes tennis.

Add text:

She believe^s she can win.

See all Proofreader's Marks on page ix.

Name ______________________ Date ______________

26 What Forms of *Be* Are Used in the Present?

Am, *Is*, and *Are*

- Use the form of the verb **be** that matches the subject.

  I **am** happy for Moni.

  She **is** the oldest child in a family of five children.

  Her sisters **are** young.

  They **are** in grade school.

  We **are** happy that Moni will go to college.

Present Tense Forms of *Be*
I **am**
he, she, or it **is**
we, you, or they **are**

- Use **not** after the **verbs am**, **is**, and **are** to make a sentence negative. The short form of **is not** is **isn't**. The short form of **are not** is **aren't**.

  1. Moni **is not** nervous about going to college.

     Moni **isn't** nervous about going to college.

  2. Her sisters **are not** in high school yet.

     Her sisters **aren't** in high school yet.

Try It

A. Complete each sentence with the correct form of be.

1. Moni's parents ___are___ (am / are) proud of her.
2. Moni ___is___ (am / is) the first person in her family to go to college.
3. We ___are___ (is / are) delighted that she is going to college.
4. You ___are___ (am / are) happy for her, aren't you?
5. Moni ___isn't___ (isn't / aren't) worried about tough classes.
6. She ___is___ (am / is) committed to succeeding.

B. **Draw lines to logically connect the words in the first column to those in the second column.**

7. Moni's sisters	aren't surprised by Moni's good grades.
8. Moni	is busy preparing for college.
9. All of Moni's friends	isn't registered for a local college.
10. Her teachers	are also busy preparing for college this fall.
11. She	are hopeful about going to college, too.

Write It

C. **Your friend wants to do something that no one in his or her family has ever done before. Answer the questions about being the first to do something. Use present tense forms of be.**

12. Is his or her family supportive about this dream? How? My friend's family ______________________________.

13. What do your friend's parents expect from their son or daughter? They ______________________________.

14. What is it like to be the first at something? It ______________________________.

15. Are you supportive of your friend? How? ______________________________

D. **(16–20) Write at least five sentences about something that you would like to be the first to do. Use present tense forms of be.**

____

____

____

____

____

____

Name ______________________ Date ____________

27 How Do You Show That an Action Is in Process?

Use *Am*, *Is*, or *Are* Plus the *-ing* Form of the Verb.

- The **present progressive** form of the verb ends in **-ing**.
- Use **am**, **is**, or **are** plus a **main verb** with **-ing** to show that an action is in the process of happening. The **helping verb** must agree with the subject.

  I **am helping** Ms. Torre.
  The group **is learning** how to save water.
  They **are learning** how much water these plants need.
  Ms. Torre **is teaching** us to use different plants to save water.

Try It

A. Complete each sentence. Write the correct present progressive verb form.

1. Ms. Torre ___is designing___ a garden that needs very little water.
   am designing / is designing
2. She ___is showing___ us how to use plants that grow well here.
   are showing / is showing
3. The neighbors ___are planting___ flowers that can survive without rain.
   is planting / are planting
4. I ___am following___ a plan for the tall grass plants that will improve the area.
   am following / are following
5. These plants ___are recreating___ the prairie land that existed years ago.
   is recreating / are recreating

B. Complete each sentence. Write the present progressive form of the verb in parentheses.

6. I ___am discovering___ plants that will conserve water. **(discover)**
7. Ms. Torre ___is saving___ the city money with these plants, too. **(save)**
8. She ___is sharing___ new techniques with the city planners. **(share)**
9. The plants ___are growing___ in a healthy way. **(grow)**
10. They ___are filling___ the city park with beauty. **(fill)**

Write It

C. **You want to improve the environment. What is your plan to help save water and trees, or to recycle? Use present progressive verb forms.**

11. What are you doing in your school or neighborhood to help the environment? I ____.

12. How are people in your area trying to help the environment? ____

13. Describe an animal or a plant that is in danger of becoming extinct. What are people doing to help change this situation? ____

D. **(14–16) Write at least three sentences about ways that people are improving the environment. Use present progressive verb forms.**

____

____

____

____

____

Edit It

E. **(17–20) Edit the community flyer. Fix the four errors in present progressive verb forms.**

Logan Square Garden Club is learning about water!
You [are] going to help us save water.
We are give[ing] classes on Saturday. We am [are] teaching about good plants for our area.
You are help[ing] your town if you conserve.

Proofreader's Marks

Add text:
You [are] saving water.

Change text:
I am hope [ing] that you will help.

See all Proofreader's Marks on page ix.

Name ______________________ Date ____________

28 What Forms of *Have* Are Used in the Present?

Have and Has

Use the form of the verb **have** that matches the subject.

- I **have** a copy of the magazine.
- Do you **have** this fabric?
- Maritza **has** a sewing machine.
- She **has** a book of designs.
- Designers **have** a lot of ideas.
- We all **have** different styles.

Present Tense Forms of *Have*
I **have**
he, she, or it **has**
we, you, or they **have**

Try It

A. Complete each sentence with the correct form of have.

1. Maritza ___has___ (have / has) a lot of fashion magazines.

2. Do you ___have___ (have / has) a copy of the September issue?

3. Maritza ___has___ (have / has) a new way to make her designs.

4. Now she ___has___ (have / has) a plan to use her sewing machine.

B. Complete each sentence with have or has.

5. We ___have___ an idea for Maritza about the fashion design group.

6. The fashion designers ___have___ a lot of experience.

7. One fashion buyer ___has___ an interest in Maritza's work.

8. Maritza's designs ___have___ a unique look.

Write It

C. Answer the questions about reaching a goal. Use present tense forms of **have**.

9. What talent or skill do you have that you would like to develop? ______

10. Who do you know who can inspire and motivate you? ______

11. What resources do you have that will help you along the way? ______

12. What do other people have that will help you face the challenge? ______

D. (13–16) Write at least four sentences about a hero or role model who has inspired you. Use present tense forms of **have** in some of your sentences.

______

Edit It

E. (17–20) Edit the letter. Fix the four errors with **have** and **has**.

Dear Uncle Martin,

Mom has a photo album with pictures of you. It ~~have~~ has several pictures of you at the top of mountains you climbed. She ~~have~~ has pride in your achievements as a mountain climber. You have a lot of courage to climb those peaks. Thanks to you, I am inspired to go after my dreams. I ~~has~~ have a desire to become a climber, too.

Andrew

Proofreader's Marks

Add text:
You have a goal to rock climb.

Change text:
Pedro ~~have~~ has the right gear for you.

See all Proofreader's Marks on page ix.

Name ______________________________ Date ______________

29 What Forms of *Do* Are Used in the Present?

Do and *Does*

- Use the form of **do** that matches the subject. You can use **do** as a **main verb** or as a **helping verb**.

  Jorge **does** three sports during the week.
  We **do admire** him.
  Our workouts **do help** us.
  They **do prepare** our bodies for the competition.
  We always **do** our best.

Present Tense Forms of *Do*
I **do**
he, she, or it **does**
we, you, or they **do**

- The short form of **does not** is **doesn't.**
- The short form of **do not** is **don't.**

1. He **does not** accept failure.
He **doesn't** accept failure.

2. They **do not** expect him to win.
They **don't** expect him to win.

Try It

A. Complete the sentence with the correct form of do.

1. Jorge ___does___ his workout routine every day. (do / does)

2. His friends ___do___ some of the exercises with him. (do / does)

3. They ___don't___ work out every day. (doesn't / don't)

4. Jorge ___doesn't___ miss a day. (doesn't / don't)

5. We ___do___ admire how he pushes himself. (do / does)

6. Jorge ___does___ enjoy this new challenge. (do / does)

7. The training is intense, but it ___doesn't___ bother him. (doesn't / don't)

B. Complete the sentence with **do**, **does**, **don't**, or **doesn't**.

8. Jorge ___does___ fifty push-ups every morning.

9. He ___does___ his strength training every day after school.

10. The biking ___doesn't___ worry him because the course is easy.

11. The swimming ___does___ tire him after so many laps.

12. Jorge's coach ___doesn't___ want him to injure himself.

13. Since he started this challenge, Jorge's teachers ___don't___ think he is the same person.

14. Jorge ___does___ enjoy this new way of testing his abilities.

15. We ___do___ hope he wins the event.

Write It

C. Answer the questions about challenging yourself. Use do and does in some of your sentences.

16. What do you do to push yourself to exceed expectations? I ______________________
____.

17. What do you do to prepare for the challenge? ______________________
____

18. What do other people do to help you? ______________________
____

D. (19–20) Write at least two sentences about how you test your abilities and push yourself to succeed. Use present tense forms of **do**.

____
____
____
____

Name ______________________ Date ____________

30 Use Verbs to Talk About the Present

Remember: The verbs **be**, **have**, and **do** each have more than one form in the present. Use the form that goes with the subject.

Forms of *Be*	**Forms of *Have***	**Forms of *Do***
I **am**	I **have**	I **do**
he, she, or it **is**	he, she, or it **has**	he, she, or it **does**
we, you, or they **are**	we, you, or they **have**	we, you, or they **do**

Try It

A. Complete the sentence. Write the correct form of the verb.

1. I ____am____ reading a book about an explorer.
am / is

2. He ____is____ famous for traveling to Antarctica.
are / is

3. The explorer and his crew ____have____ many adventures along the way.
have / has

4. I ____have____ a dream to become an explorer, too.
have / has

B. Complete each sentence with the correct present tense form of the verb in parentheses.

5. I ____do____ like to travel to unusual places. **(do)**

6. An explorer ____has____ a life of adventure. **(have)**

7. In the book, the crew ____has____ an accident. **(have)**

8. I ____do____ understand that a journey can be dangerous. **(do)**

9. We ____have____ a lot to learn from modern explorers. **(have)**

Write It

C. You admire a person for something he or she does that makes a positive change in the world. What can you do to honor this person? Answer the questions. Use present tense forms of the verbs **be**, **have**, or **do** in some of your sentences.

10. What does this person do that inspires you? ______________________________

____

11. What qualities and experience does this person have that make you admire him or her?

____

12. What are you doing now to honor what this person does? ______________________

____

D. (13–16) Write at least four sentences about someone you admire. Use present tense forms of the verbs **be**, **have**, or **do** in some of your sentences.

____

____

____

____

____

Edit It

E. (17–20) Edit the postcard. Fix the four mistakes in verb forms.

Dear Natalie,

I am eager to meet the explorer this weekend at the book signing. As you know, his writings ~~is~~ are an inspiration to me. He ~~do~~ does not let fear get in the way of his goal. I already ~~has~~ have a copy of his latest book. I know that you ~~has~~ have great respect for this man, too. I will meet you at the bookstore.

See you soon,

Brigitte

Proofreader's Marks

Change text:
I ~~has~~ have a new book.

See all Proofreader's Marks on page ix.

Name ______________________________ Date ______________

Capitalize Job Titles, Courtesy Titles, and Family Titles

- **Job titles** should be capitalized when they come before a person's name. When they follow the person's name or the word **the**, they are not capitalized.

  Coach Jones

  Mr. Jones, **the coach**

  Mr. David Jones is **the coach**.

- **Courtesy titles**, such as **Mr.**, **Mrs.**, and **Ms.** should always be capitalized.

  Mr. Santoro's rules

  Ms. Hansen's class

- **Family titles** should be capitalized when they are used in place of a person's name. When they follow a possessive adjective, they are not capitalized.

  I helped **Dad** pack the car for our trip.

  I helped **my dad** pack the car for our trip.

Try It

Proofreader's Marks

Capitalize:

This is principal Mendez.

Do not capitalize:

Dr. Mendez is the Principal.

See all Proofreader's Marks on page ix.

A. Use proofreader's marks to correct the capitalization error in each sentence.

1. Our high school soccer coach is mr. Turner.
2. I asked coach Turner if I could try out for the soccer team.
3. The Principal, Ms. Morgan, took me to the soccer field.
4. I saw mom after tryouts and told her the good news.
5. My Dad was excited to hear that I made the team.

Name ____________________ Date ____________

Edit and Proofread

Use the Dash Correctly

- Use a dash or pair of dashes to show a sudden change in thought or speech.

  They got me a magazine that's all about—**you guessed it**—soccer.

- Do not overuse dashes. For example, dashes should not be used in place of periods, commas, and other appropriate punctuation.

  Incorrect: I nodded—ran onto the field—and found the team captain.

  Correct: I nodded, **ran onto the field**, and found the team captain.

Try It

A. **(6–10) Edit the journal entry. Find and fix the five punctuation mistakes.**

October 20

Today was the day of the big game. No one—not even the principal—thought we'd make it this far. I couldn't believe it—the state championships! I put on my uniform, grabbed my water bottle, and headed out to the field. All eyes were on us. We were here to win, but we also knew that trying our best was the real win.

Proofreader's Marks

Add a dash:

Suddenly, I saw what it was—a soccer ball.

Replace dashes:

Next, I took a deep breath.

B. **Rewrite each sentence using a dash or pair of dashes.**

11. Mr. Turner he's the soccer coach let me try out.

Mr. Turner—he's the soccer coach—let me try out.

12. I ran down the field with the ball passing everyone and kicked the ball right into the net.

I ran down the field with the ball—passing everyone—and kicked the ball right into the net.

Name ______________________ Date ____________

Edit and Proofread

Check Your Spelling

Homonyms are words that sound alike but have different meanings and spellings. Spell these homonyms correctly when you proofread.

Homonyms and Their Meanings	Examples
to (preposition) = toward, in the direction of	I am going **to** soccer tryouts.
two (noun) = one more than one	I scored **two** goals.
too (adverb) = also	Do you want to play soccer, **too**?
your (adjective) = belonging to you	Can you show us **your** soccer skills?
you're (contraction) = you are	**You're** going to be late for tryouts.

Try It

A. Complete each sentence. Use the correct homonym.

13. On the way ___to___ (to / two / too) tryouts, the family car broke down.

14. We waited ___two___ (to / two / too) hours for a tow truck.

15. "___You're___ (Your / You're) going to be late for the tryouts," my mother said.

16. After what seemed liked hours, we finally made it ___to___ (to / two / too) the school.

B. (17–19) Write a short paragraph about an obstacle or challenge that you overcame. Use at least three homonyms in your paragraph.

____

____

____

____

____

Name ______________________ Date ____________

Edit and Proofread

Use the Verbs *Can*, *Could*, *May*, and *Might* Correctly

- Use **may**, **might**, or **could** to tell about a possibility.
  We **might win** the championship.
  We **may** be the next champions!
  We **could become** the best team in the state.
- Use **may** to tell that an action is permitted, or allowed.
  Coach said, "If you finish your laps, you **may leave**."
- Use **can** or **could** to tell about an ability.
  Melissa **can kick** the farthest.
  She **could kick** well last year, too.

Try It

A. (20–25) **Complete the story with can, could, may, and might.**

I'll never forget that day when I auditioned for the Paul Robeson School of the Performing Arts. I thought I ___might___ get admitted to the program, but I wasn't sure. I was nervous. Sure, I ___can___ speak two languages, but in that first moment on stage, I ___could___ not remember a syllable of either one.

"You ___may___ begin now, Anthony," Ms. Gupta said. I looked up and saw a row of teachers waiting for me to begin. Then I remembered what my teacher Mrs. Rico always said. She said, "Whenever you get nervous, you ___might___ want to take a deep breath." So I cleared my throat and took a deep breath. Ever since I was old enough to talk, I ___could___ act. This is what I love to do! I started to speak, and my nervousness slowly disappeared. Finally, I bowed.

That day, I overcame my stage fright—and I got admitted to the school!

Name ______________________ Date ______________

31 How Do You Show That an Action Already Happened?

Add *-ed* to the Verb.

- Action in the **present tense** happens now or on a regular basis.
- Action in the **past tense** happened earlier.

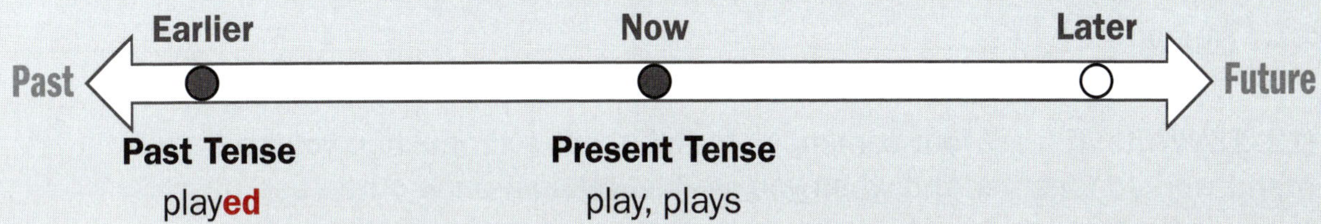

Add **-ed** to most verbs when you talk about a past action. If there is more than one verb in a sentence, they must all be in the same tense.

1. Linh and Jess **play** music together. They **played** in a concert yesterday.
2. They often **encounter** new songs, **learn** them, and **play** them. They **encountered** one, **learned** it, and **played** it last week.

Try It

A. Complete each sentence. Write the past tense of each verb in parentheses.

1. The director of the youth orchestra displayed a poster. **(display)**
2. The orchestra needed new members. **(need)**
3. The director wanted musicians to audition. **(want)**
4. Linh and Jess both looked and talked at the poster. **(look) (talk)**
5. They discussed trying out and decided to do so. **(discuss)**

B. Write the present tense or past tense of the verb in parentheses.

6. Earlier this morning, Linh and Jess walked to the tryouts. **(walk)**
7. A few hours ago, they both auditioned for the orchestra. **(audition)**
8. They performed very well and were proud of themselves. **(perform)**

Write It

C. Imagine that two friends ran against each other for student council president. One won, and the other lost. Write sentences about what probably happened after the election. Use the past tense of the verb in parentheses.

9. **(talk)** They probably ____.

10. **(learn)** They ____.

11. **(remain)** They ____.

D. (12–15) Write at least four sentences to tell about a time when you and a friend worked together and when you worked against each other. Use past tense verbs that end in **-ed**. In one sentence, use three past tense verbs.

____

____

____

____

____

Edit It

E. (16–20) Edit the journal entry. Fix five mistakes with verbs.

May 10

Right now, I really need to find a job. Yesterday, I filled out an application. The job ~~sound~~ sounded interesting. My best friend applied for the same job! That was not good! Earlier this morning, the managers ~~call~~ called my friend and ~~offer~~ offered him the job. A few minutes ago, we ~~talk~~ talked about it. We're still friends, but I still ~~needed~~ need to find a job.

Proofreader's Marks

Change text:

Yesterday, I ~~want~~ wanted that job.

See all Proofreader's Marks on page ix.

Name ______________________ Date ____________

32 Can You Just Add *-ed* to Form a Verb in the Past?

Not Always

Most verbs end with **-ed** to show the past tense. Sometimes you have to change the spelling of the verb before you add **-ed**. Follow these rules:

1. If a verb ends in silent **e**, drop the **e**. Then add **-ed**.
   Josh decid**ed** to play for the Blazers. **(decide)**
   Scott's team compet**ed** against the Blazers. **(compete)**
2. Some one-syllable verbs end in one vowel and one consonant. Double the consonant before you add **-ed**.
   Josh and Scott jogg**ed** together. **(jog)**
   Then they batt**ed** the ball around. **(bat)**

Try It

A. Complete each sentence. Write the past tense of the verb in parentheses.

1. Scott and Josh joked about the big game. **(joke)**
2. Each boy hoped his team would win. **(hope)**
3. They patted each other on the back. **(pat)**
4. They even grinned at each other. **(grin)**
5. Then the boys waved and joined their own teams. **(wave)**

B. (6–10) Complete each sentence. Choose a verb from the box and use its past tense form.

grab	raise	slug	smile	tag

Josh raised the bat into position. He slugged the ball. Then Scott grabbed it. Scott tagged Josh out at first base. Scott smiled because his team won the game.

Write It

C. Answer each question about competing against a friend. Use the past tense.

11. When did you compete against a friend? I ______________________________.

12. How did the competition end? ______________________________

13. Did you like the competition? ______________________________

14. What did you and your friend plan to do next? ______________________________

D. (15–18) Imagine that two friends competed against each other in a game of basketball. Write at least four sentences about the competition. Use the past tense of these verbs: dribble, move, clap, drop.

____

____

____

____

____

Edit It

E. (19–25) Edit this letter. Fix seven mistakes with verbs.

Dear Scott,

Do you remember that last game we played before I ~~move~~ moved? I ~~loveed~~ loved playing against your team. I ~~line~~ lined out to you, but I also ~~tag~~ tagged you out! Do you remember when Ross ~~droped~~ dropped that fly ball? We ~~ussed~~ used to have a lot of fun, didn't we? I miss those days. I am sorry I ~~moveed~~ moved away.

Your friend,

Josh

Proofreader's Marks

Change text: We ~~competted~~ competed well.

See all Proofreader's Marks on page ix.

Name ______________________________ Date ______________

33 When Do You Use *Was* and *Were*?

When You Tell About the Past

The verb **be** has special forms to tell about the present and the past.

Past ← Earlier — Now — Later → Future

Past Tense	Present Tense
I **was**	I **am**
you **were**	you **are**
he, she, or it **was**	he, she, or it **is**
we **were**	we **are**
they **were**	they **are**

Present: Josie **is** at Alberto's party.
Past: She **was** not there last year.

Present: Josie and Alberto **are** good friends now.
Past: They **were** not good friends last year.

Try It

A. Rewrite each sentence. Use the past tense of the verb.

1. I am Josie's good friend. I was Josie's good friend.
2. Josie and Alberto are good friends. Josie and Alberto were good friends.
3. Alberto is not my friend. Alberto was not my friend.
4. Josie is one of the kids invited to Alberto's party. Josie was one of the kids invited to Alberto's party.
5. I am not on the guest list. I was not on the guest list.

B. Complete each sentence. Write **was**, **were**, or **are**.

6. Last week, my feelings ___were___ hurt.

7. Then Josie ___was___ thoughtful of my feelings.

8. Her friends ___were___ thoughtful, too.

9. They ___were___ nice when they talked to Alberto.

10. He ___was___ happy to invite me to his party.

11. I ___was___ glad to be invited.

12. Now Alberto, Josie, and I ___are___ all good friends.

Write It

C. Complete the sentences to tell about a time you felt left out. Use **was** or **were** in each sentence.

13. I ______________________________.

14. My friends ______________________________.

15. We all ______________________________.

16. It ______________________________.

D. (17–20) Write at least four sentences to tell about a time a friend of yours was left out. What did you do? Use **was** or **were** in each sentence.

____

____

____

____

____

Name ______________________ Date ______________

34 When Do You Use *Had*?

When You Tell About the Past

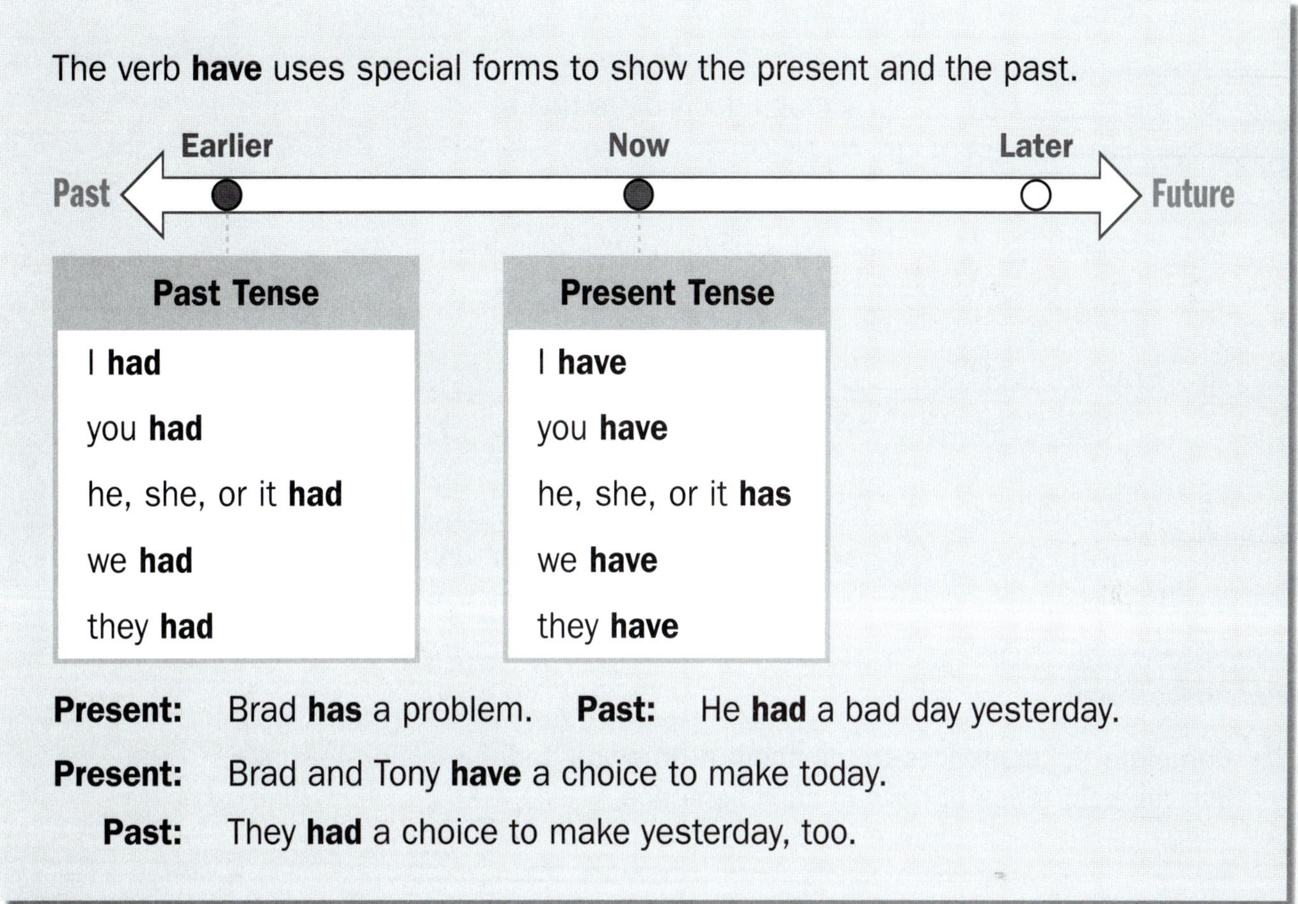

Try It

A. Rewrite each sentence. Use the past tense of the verb.

1. Brad and Tony have a great friendship. Brad and Tony had a great friendship.

2. They accidentally damage some school property on Monday. They accidentally damaged some school property on Monday.

3. On Tuesday, the principal has Tony in his office. On Tuesday, the principal had Tony in his office.

4. Tony has a chance to protect Brad. Tony had a chance to protect Brad.

B. Write **have** or **has** to complete each sentence. Then rewrite the sentence in the past tense.

5. Brad has a strong sense of loyalty to his friend.
Brad had a strong sense of loyalty to his friend.

6. He has a tough decision to make.
He had a tough decision to make.

7. His parents have some advice for him.
His parents had some advice for him.

8. Brad has good advice.
Brad had good advice.

9. Brad and Tony have detention together for a week.
Brad and Tony had detention together for a week.

Write It

C. Complete the sentences to tell about a time you had a decision to make. Use the past tense of **have** in each sentence.

10. I ______________________________
______________________________.

11. My friends ______________________________
______________________________.

12. We ______________________________
______________________________.

D. (13–15) Write at least three sentences about loyalty to friends. Use **have**, **has**, and **had**.

____
____
____
____
____

Name ______________________ Date ____________

35 Use Verb Tenses

Remember: You have to change the verb to show the past tense. Be sure to use the same tense for all verbs in the same sentence.

Add **-ed** to most verbs. You may need to make a spelling change before you add **-ed**.

Present Tense	Past Tense
look, looks	looked
want, wants	wanted
hop, hops	hopped
use, uses	used

Use special forms for the past tense of **be** and **have**.

Forms of *Be*	
Present Tense	**Past Tense**
am, is, are	was, were

Forms of *Have*	
Present Tense	**Past Tense**
have, has	had

Try It

A. Write the correct form of the verbs to complete the sentences.

1. Last week, the teacher asked (ask / asked) Ana and Jo to judge the art contest.
2. By the end of the week, the girls had (have / had) to decide what to do.
3. Right now, they are (are / were) judges.
4. A few days ago, their friends entered (enter / entered) their art in the contest.
5. Afterward, their friends joked (joke / joked) about being friends with the judges!

B. Complete each sentence. Write the past tense of the verb in parentheses.

6–7. Ana and Jo needed and hoped to be fair. **(need) (hope)**

8. They skipped over all the artists' names. **(skip)**

Write It

C. Complete the sentences to tell about a contest in which students had to choose between loyalty and fairness. Use the past tense of the verbs in parentheses.

9. **(judge)** Students ______________________________.

10. **(be)** The contest ______________________________.

11. **(have)** Everyone ______________________________.

12. **(grin)** The winner ______________________________.

D. (13–16) Write at least four sentences about a time you had to choose between loyalty and fairness. Use past tense verbs, including the past tense of **be** and **have**, in your sentences. In one sentence, use three past tense verbs.

____

____

____

____

____

____

Edit It

E. (17–25) Edit the student newspaper article about the art contest. Fix eight mistakes with verbs.

Art Contest Winners Chosen

Last week, our school sponsored an art contest. All the students ~~has~~ had a chance to enter. The art teachers ~~invitted~~ invited students to judge the contest. The student judges ~~was~~ were fair. They ~~pushhed~~ pushed aside their loyalty to their friends and ~~base~~ based their decisions on the quality of the art. The teachers ~~snaped~~ snapped this photo of the judges and winners. The contest ~~is~~ was a success. The winners ~~was~~ were happy and ~~smiles~~ smiled to show it..

Proofreader's Marks

Change text:

I ~~were~~ was a judge in the art show.

See all Proofreader's Marks on page ix.

Name ____________________ Date ____________

36 How Do You Show That an Action Already Happened?

Change the Verb.

Add **-ed** to most verbs to show that an action already happened.
Use special past tense forms for **irregular verbs.**

Present	Past	Example in the Past
am, is, are	was, were	Susan **was** a piano teacher.
say	said	My friend **said** she was a good teacher.
do, does	did	She **did** a great job teaching him to play.
have, has	had	My friend **had** fun studying with Susan.
wake	woke	He **woke** up every morning and practiced.
hear	heard	Sometimes I **heard** him from next door.
ring	rang	When my alarm clock **rang**, I was already awake.

Try It

A. Rewrite each sentence. Use the past tense of the verb.

1. Susan hears about a job at the music store. Susan heard about a job at the music store.
2. She is a great candidate for the job. She was a great candidate for the job.
3. Susan has years of teaching experience. Susan had years of teaching experience.
4. My friend rings up the store on the telephone. My friend rang up the store on the telephone.
5. He says that she would be a great teacher. He said that she would be a great teacher.

B. Complete each sentence with the past tense of a verb from the box. Use **be** two times.

be	do	have	hear	ring	say	wake

6. The telephone at Susan's house rang.
7. Susan heard it from outside.
8. The manager at the music store had bad news for her.
9. He said someone else got the job.
10. That applicant was a friend of the manager.
11. The call woke Susan up to the realities of life.
12. Susan did everything she could.
13. Were things fair when a friend of the manager got the job?

Write It

C. Answer the questions to give your opinions about Susan's situation. Use the past tense of irregular verbs.

14. What loyalties did the store manager have? The store manager ______________________________.
15. Was what happened to Susan fair? ______________________________
16. What do you think Susan said to the manager? ______________________________

D. (17–20) Write at least four sentences to tell how loyalties helped you or kept you from getting something you wanted. Use the past tense of at least four irregular verbs.

____
____
____
____

Name ________________ Date ________

37 How Do You Show That an Action Already Happened?

Change the Verb.

Add -ed to most verbs to show that an action already happened.
Use special past tense forms for **irregular verbs.**

Present	Past	Example in the Past
feel	felt	Carlos **felt** sad when Oscar ignored him on the basketball court.
go, goes	went	Carlos and Oscar **went** to school together.
get	got	Carlos **got** a strange feeling from Oscar whenever he saw him.
know	knew	He **knew** that Oscar wasn't being nice.
meet	met	Recently, Carlos **met** Eduardo.
tell	told	Eduardo **told** Carlos about a good movie.
see	saw	The boys **saw** the movie together.

Try It

A. Complete each sentence. Write the past tense form of the verb in parentheses.

1. Carlos ___knew___ that something was wrong. **(know)**
2. Oscar ___saw___ him and didn't say hello. **(see)**
3. Oscar ___went___ off with some new friends. **(go)**
4. Carlos ___got___ the message. **(get)**
5. He ___told___ Eduardo that old friends were not always loyal friends. **(tell)**

B. (6–12) **Complete the paragraph with past tense verbs.** Possible responses:

Carlos knew that Eduardo was a better friend than Oscar. Even though he only met Eduardo a few weeks ago, Carlos felt closer to him. Carlos and Eduardo saw each other a lot. They told each other their problems and helped each other out. They got along better than Carlos and Oscar. Carlos and Oscar went their separate ways. Carlos learned that old friends were not always best friends.

Write It

C. **Answer the questions to tell about a time when an old friend was not a good friend. Use the past tense of irregular verbs.**

13. What did your friend tell you? My friend ______________________________.

14. How did you feel? I ______________________________.

15. What did you know? I ______________________________.

16. Where did you go? I ______________________________.

D. (17–20) **Write at least four sentences that tell about an old friend and a new friend. Use the past tense of at least four irregular verbs from the chart on page 81.**

____

____

____

____

____

Name ______________________________ Date ______________

38 How Do You Show That an Action Was in Process?

Use *Was* or *Were* Plus the *-ing* Form of the Verb.

- Sometimes you want to show that an action was happening over a period of time in the past. Use the past progressive form.
- To form the past progressive, use the helping verb **was** or **were** plus a main verb that ends in **-ing**. The **helping verb** must agree with the subject.

  Julio **was standing** outside the restaurant.
  Inside, the waiter **was serving** a customer.
  Other people **were sitting** patiently.
  They **were becoming** impatient, though.

Try It

A. Complete each sentence. Write the past progressive form of the verb in parentheses.

1. Julio was trying out the new restaurant. **(try)**
2. He was hoping the food would taste really good. **(hope)**
3. Many customers were waiting to be seated. **(wait)**
4. Two of the owner's friends were stopping in at the restaurant. **(stop)**
5. The owner was seating them right away. **(seat)**

B. Choose a verb from the box to complete each sentence. Use the past progressive form.

begin	feel	ignore	leave

6. Julio was feeling angry.
7. Some people were leaving the line to go somewhere else to eat.
8. One customer was beginning to complain.
9. The owner was ignoring his complaints.

Write It

C. **Imagine that you were waiting in line at the restaurant. Answer the questions about your experience. Use the past progressive form of verbs in your answers.**

10. What were you doing while you were waiting? ______________________

____

11. How were you feeling when the owner's friends were seated first? ______________________

____

12. Was the owner treating anyone fairly? What was he doing? ______________________

____

D. **(13–16) Write at least four sentences about a time you were treated either fairly or unfairly at a store or a restaurant. Use the past progressive form of a verb in each sentence.**

____

____

____

____

____

Edit It

E. **(17–20) Edit the restaurant review below. Fix four past progressive verbs.**

Danny's Fish Fry

I ate at the fish restaurant last night—Danny's Fish Fry. The experience was a huge disappointment. The food was good, but the service was not. The owner was giving preferential treatment to some customers. New customers ~~were get~~ were getting angry. They ^were looking at their watches. These customers ~~was wish~~ were wishing they had eaten someplace else. Other customers ~~was~~ were waiting to be served their meals. It is important to treat loyal customers well, but it is important to treat new customers well, too!

Proofreader's Marks

Add text:
We ^were hoping for a good meal.

Change text:
The owner ~~were snub~~ was snubbing us.

See all Proofreader's Marks on page ix.

Name ______________________ Date ____________

39 How Do You Tell About the Future?

Use *Will* Before the Verb.

- The **future tense** of a verb shows that an action will happen later.

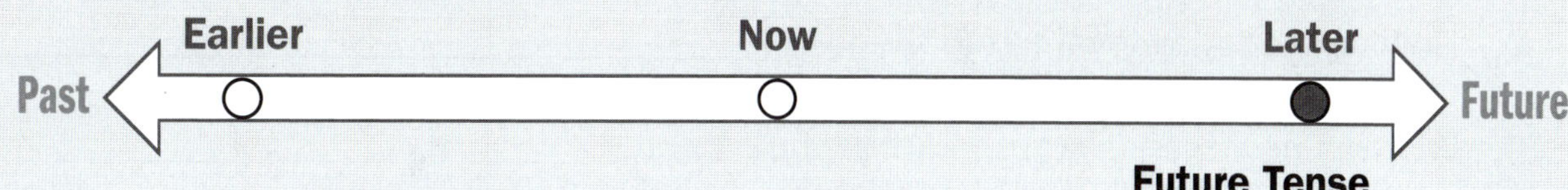

To form the future tense, use **will** before the main verb.

Tim **will move** to a neighboring town.

You can also use **am**, **is**, or **are** plus **going to** before the main verb.

He **is going to make** new friends.

If **will** or **am**, **is**, or **are** plus **going to** comes before the first verb in a series, all three verbs are in the future tense.

He **is going to keep** his old friends, **make** new ones, and **enjoy** them all.

Try It

A. **Write the future tense of the verb in parentheses to complete each sentence. More than one answer is possible.** Possible responses:

1. Tim will live close to his new school. **(live)**
2. His old friends will visit him in his new home. **(visit)**
3. Tim is going to drive back to see them, too. **(drive)**
4. Tim will get to know new friends, too. **(get)**
5. He will want to have friends in his new school. **(want)**

B. **Write a future tense verb to complete each sentence.** Possible responses:

6. Tim will stay loyal to his old friends and text them often.
7. He is going to introduce them to his new friends.

Write It

C. Imagine that you are going to move to a new town and go to a new school. Answer the questions. Use future tense verbs.

8. How will you meet new friends? I ______________________.

9. How will you stay loyal to old friends? I ______________________.

10. Why will new friends want to know you? They ______________________
______________________.

D. (11–12) Now write at least two sentences to tell about something you will do with your friends. Use a future tense verb in each sentence. Use three future tense verbs in one of your sentences.

____
____
____
____

Edit It

E. (13–20) Edit the journal entry. Fix eight mistakes with verbs. There is more than one way to make each correction.

Possible responses:

May 16

Tomorrow I will have a good time. I ~~got~~ am going to get together with my friends. We will go on a long hike together. Both my old friends and my new friends will hike with me. We ~~climbed~~ will climb to the top of a mountain and ~~will~~ view the valley. Then, we are going to eat a picnic lunch. I ~~enjoyed~~ will enjoy the day because all my loyal friends ~~had~~ will have fun together.

Proofreader's Marks

Add text:
I will take plenty of water with me.

Change text:
Tomorrow, I ~~went~~ will go on a hike.

See all Proofreader's Marks on page ix.

Name ______________________ Date ____________

40 Use Verb Tenses

Remember: You have to change the verb to show when an action happens. The action can happen in the **present**, **past**, or **future**.

The **tense** of a verb tells when an action happens.

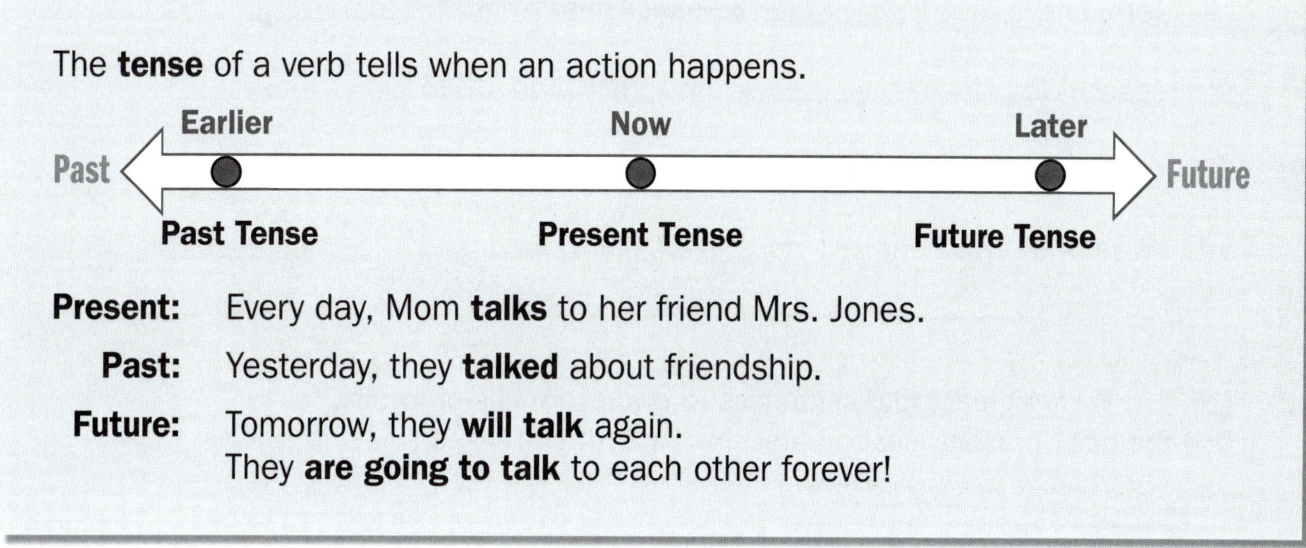

Present: Every day, Mom **talks** to her friend Mrs. Jones.

Past: Yesterday, they **talked** about friendship.

Future: Tomorrow, they **will talk** again.
They **are going to talk** to each other forever!

Try It

A. Complete each sentence. Write the correct tense of the verb in parentheses.

1. Mom ___met___ Mrs. Jones years ago. **(past of meet)**

2. They ___went___ to kindergarten together. **(past of go)**

3. Now, Mrs. Jones ___has___ a new home that is far away. **(present of have)**

4. She ___is___ still Mom's loyal friend, though. **(present of be)**

5. Just yesterday, Mom ___was telling___ me about the friendship. **(past progressive of tell)**

6–7. She ___said___ that Mrs. Jones ___will visit___ us later this year. **(past of say; future of visit)**

B. Complete each sentence. Write a verb in the tense in parentheses. Possible responses:

8. Yesterday, I ___saw___ my loyal friend Jenna and ___had___ fun. **(past)**

9. We ___were riding___ our bicycles together. **(past progressive)**

10. I hope that Jenna and I ___will remain___ loyal friends forever. **(future)**

Write It

C. Complete the sentences about a loyal friend. Use the verb tenses given in parentheses.

11. **(present)** I _______________ a loyal friend named _______________.

12. **(past)** We _______________ a long time ago when _______________.

13. **(past progressive)** Just yesterday, my friend and I _______________.

14. **(future)** In the future, I hope that my friend and I _______________

_______________.

D. (15–18) Write at least four sentences to give examples of loyalty. Use the past, present, past progressive, and future tenses.

____

____

____

____

____

Edit It

E. (19–25) Edit the letter below. Fix seven mistakes. Possible responses:

Dear Amanda,

Yesterday, Marie was asking about our long and loyal friendship. I ~~telled~~ told her about how we ~~meet~~ met when we ~~was~~ were in kindergarten. Now, forty years later, we ~~was~~ are still good friends. Last night, I ~~go~~ was going through our high school yearbook. How young we ~~look~~ looked back then! I'm looking forward to your visit next month. We will have a lot to talk about then.

Love,

Shirley

Proofreader's Marks

Add text:

Loyal friends are important.

Change text:

Yesterday, I ~~write~~ wrote to my good friend.

See all Proofreader's Marks on page ix.

Name ______________________ Date ______________

41 How Do Nouns Work in a Sentence?

They Can Be the Subject or the Object.

- Nouns can be the **subject** of a sentence.

  My **friend** lives in the United States now.
  subject

- Nouns can also be the **object** of an action verb. To find the object, turn the verb into a question such as: "Visit whom?" Your answer is the object.

  My friend's parents visit my **friend** every year.
  verb object

- Many English sentences follow this pattern: **subject → verb → object**.

  Marissa has **loyalty** to both countries.
  subject verb object

  Sometimes world events influence her **loyalties**.
  subject verb object

Try It

A. Read each sentence. Write **subject** if the underlined noun is a subject. Write **object** if it is an object.

1. The country where Marissa was born suffers from poverty. subject
2. Many people do not have enough food to eat. object
3. Marissa makes donations to charities. object
4. Her generous donations help many people get food. subject
5. Marissa's loyalty to that country helps many people. object

B. Write a noun to complete each sentence. Then circle the subjects and underline the objects. Possible responses:

6. My friend feels loyalty to the United States, too.
7. Sometimes Marissa dislikes the politics.
8. Events happening around the world influence those politics.

Write It

C. **Answer the questions about world events and loyalties. Circle each subject and underline each object.**

9. What world events affect the world today? ______________________________

____

10. How do the events influence people? ______________________________

____

11. How do the events change your loyalties? ______________________________

____

D. **(12–14) Sometimes wars affect people's loyalty. Write at least three sentences about the Revolutionary War, the Civil War, or another war. Tell how the war might have affected loyalties. Use a subject and object in each sentence.**

____

____

____

____

____

Edit It

E. **(15–20) Edit the paragraph. Add six missing subjects or objects.** Possible responses:

The United States fought a war in Vietnam in the 1960s and 1970s. The United States sent ^troops to Vietnam. Some ^Americans disliked the ^war. They organized ^marches to protest the war. Some marchers carried ^signs expressing their beliefs. The war tested their ^loyalties to the United States government.

Proofreader's Marks

Add text:
A ^war influences loyalties.

See all Proofreader's Marks on page ix.

Name ______________________ Date ____________

42 Why Are There So Many Pronouns?

Some Work as Subjects, and Some Work as Objects.

- Use a **subject pronoun** as the subject of a sentence.

  My **mom** is running for mayor.
  She will be good for our city.

  Mom is running against **Mr. Greene.**
  He is the mayor now.

- Use an **object pronoun** as the object of the verb.

  The **election** is next month. I will watch **it** closely.

  My loyalties are with **Mom.** I support **her**.

Pronouns	
Subject	**Object**
I	me
you	you
he	him
she	her
it	it

Try It

A. Use pronouns from the chart to complete the sentences. Then underline the noun each pronoun stands for.

1. My mom will be a good mayor. ____She____ is organized and smart.
2. I respect my mom and her politics. That is why I will vote for ____her____.
3. The city needs to have a strong mayor. Mom can help ____it____ grow.
4. "Rosa, please read this. Then ____you____ might vote for Mom," I advised my friend.
5. Mr. Lopez is helping with Mom's campaign. We appreciate ____him____ very much.

B. (6–12) Write pronouns from the chart to complete the paragraph.

In the last election, Rosa voted for Mr. Greene. ____She____ supported ____him____. Now her loyalty has changed. ____It____ is with my mom. Rosa was disappointed with Mr. Greene. ____He____ did not keep his promises. "____I____ think your mom will help other residents in the city and ____me____," Rosa said. "Your mom will make this city a better place to live. That's why I support ____her____."

Write It

C. Complete the sentences. Use a subject or object pronoun in each one.

13. At school, ______________ ran for ______________. I supported ______________ because ____

____.

14. In our town, ______________ ran for ______________. I supported ______________ because ____

____.

15. In the presidential election, ______________ won. ______________________________

____.

D. (16–20) Some people have a favorite celebrity. Then their loyalty changes to a different celebrity. Write at least five sentences about a celebrity you used to like and one you like now. Use both subject and object pronouns.

____

____

____

____

____

____

Edit It

E. (21–25) Edit the news article. Fix five mistakes with pronouns.

Mrs. Sonja Nelson Wins Election

Yesterday, Mrs. Sonja Nelson won the mayoral election. It was a landslide victory. ~~Her~~ She received a large majority of the vote. Mr. Roberts was defeated. ~~Him~~ He did not receive enough votes. Mrs. Nelson thanked each and every supporter. "~~Him~~ You supported ~~it~~ me, and ~~it~~ I won," she said.

Proofreader's Marks

Change text:

Mrs. Nelson won. ~~He~~ She is our next mayor.

See all Proofreader's Marks on page ix.

Name ______________________ Date ______________

43 Do You Ever Talk About Yourself?

Then Learn to Use the Words *I* and *Me*.

Subject Pronoun: I

- Use the pronoun **I** in the **subject** of a sentence.

  I like baseball.

- In a compound subject, name yourself last.

Correct: **Dad and I** go to a game every summer.

Correct: **He and I** cheer for the same team.

Incorrect: Me and dad go to a game every summer.

Object Pronoun: me

- Use the pronoun **me** as the **object**.

  Dad takes **me** to the game.

- In a compound object, name yourself last.

Correct: My brother teases **Dad and me** about our loyalty.

Correct: He teases **him and me.**

Incorrect: He teases me and him.

Try It

A. Write I or me to complete each sentence.

1. My family and ____I____ live in Boston.

2. For that reason, ____I____ am a loyal Boston baseball fan.

3. Sometimes, my friends go to the games with ____me____.

4. The players always entertain my friends and ____me____.

5. Will ____I____ always be loyal to the Boston team?

B. (6–13) Write I or me to complete the paragraph.

Soon ____I____ will move to New York City. A New York college accepted ____me____. Right now, ____I____ do not like the New York baseball team. The team angers my friends and ____me____. My family and ____I____ wonder, though. Will ____I____ change my loyalty? Then my friends will tease ____me____. They might call ____me____ a traitor.

Write It

C. Answer the questions. Use I or me in each answer.

14. What sports team are your friends and you loyal to? ______________________

____

15. Have you ever changed your loyalty? ______________________

____

16. How does the team entertain your friends and you? ______________________

____

D. (17–20) Write at least four sentences to give your opinion about loyalty to sports teams. Use I or me in each sentence.

____

____

____

____

____

Edit It

E. (21–25) Edit the journal entry below. Fix five mistakes with pronouns.

October 15

My brother and I went to the game today. The train picked my brother and ~~I~~ me up at the station. It dropped ~~me and my brother~~ my brother and me off in Boston. ~~Me~~ I bought some popcorn. The game pleased ~~I~~ me. That's because my team won. My brother and I are loyal fans, though. We like our team whether they win or lose. ~~I and my brother~~ My brother and I will go to another game soon.

Proofreader's Marks

Change text:

~~Me and Craig~~ Craig and I are loyal fans.

See all Proofreader's Marks on page ix.

Name ______________________ Date ____________

44 Which Pronouns Refer to More Than One Person?

We, You, They, and Us, You, Them

- Use a **subject pronoun** as the subject.

  My **parents** are from Los Angeles.
  They have lived in Chicago for twenty years.
  subject

  My siblings and I are from Chicago.
  We have always lived here.
  subject

Pronouns	
Subject	**Object**
we	us
you	you
they	them

- Use an **object pronoun** as the object of the verb.

  My parents are loyal to the Los Angeles sports **teams**.
  My parents watch **them** on TV.
  object

  We are loyal to the Chicago teams. Mom and Dad take **us** to see them.
  object

Try It

A. Write pronouns from the chart to complete the sentences. Then underline the noun each pronoun stands for.

1. Mom and Dad are loyal to Los Angeles teams. ___They___ have not changed their loyalty in twenty years.

2. I try to convince Mom and Dad. I want ___them___ to change their loyalty.

3. My siblings and I have a plan. ___We___ get season tickets for our parents.

4. My parents are shocked by my siblings and me. Dad thanks ___us___.

5. My parents enjoy the games. Mom likes ___them___ so much that she becomes a fan.

6. After twenty years, my parents finally switch their loyalty. ___They___ still like Los Angeles, but Chicago is the best!

B. **Edit each sentence. Fix the plural pronouns.**

Proofreader's Marks

Change text:

We ~~Us~~ enjoy the game.

See all Proofreader's Marks on page ix.

7. My friends ask ~~we~~ [us] to go to a hockey game.
8. ~~Us~~ [We] have never really liked hockey.
9. We tell ~~they~~ [them] that we are loyal basketball fans.
10. They convince ~~we~~ [us] to go, though.
11. After the game, ~~us~~ [we] thank our friends.
12. ~~Them~~ [They] definitely changed our minds about hockey!

Write It

C. **Complete the sentences about sports loyalties. Use at least two plural subject pronouns and two plural object pronouns.**

13. My friends like ______________. ______________________________
14. My family and I prefer ______________. ______________________________
____
15. Sports are important. I ______________________________.
16. My schoolmates and I ______________. The school takes ______________
____.

D. **(17–20) Write at least four sentences to tell how friends or family members have changed sports loyalties over time. Use a plural pronoun in each sentence.**

____
____
____
____
____
____

Name ______________________________ Date ______________

45 Use Subject and Object Pronouns

Remember: Use a subject pronoun as the subject of a sentence. Use an object pronoun as the object of the verb.

Subject Pronouns	I	you	he	she	it	we	you	they
Object Pronouns	me	you	him	her	it	us	you	them

My friends and **I** love to eat ice cream in the summer. **We** go to the same ice cream stand every year. **It** has the best ice cream. Will **you** join **us** today? Tony and Alex are driving. **We** can ask **them** for a ride. **They** will take **us**.

Try It

A. Rewrite the sentences. Use pronouns for the underlined words.

1. When Tony and Alex get to the ice cream stand, Tony and Alex are surprised. When Tony and Alex get to the ice cream stand, they are surprised.

2. The ice cream stand has new owners. It has new owners.

3. Tony says, "I am surprised, but Alex and I should try the new ice cream." Tony says, "I am surprised, but we should try the new ice cream."

4. The ice cream doesn't interest Tony and Alex at all. The ice cream doesn't interest them at all.

5. Tony has been a loyal customer for years, but now Tony wants to try a new place. Tony has been a loyal customer for years, but now he wants to try a new place.

6. The next day, Alex takes Tony to try different ice cream, and it is delicious. The next day Alex takes him to try different ice cream, and it is delicious.

B. **Edit the sentences. Fix the pronouns.**

7. ~~My friends and me~~ My friends and I love Bucky's Burgers.

8. ~~Us~~ We have been loyal customers for years.

9. Now Harry's Hamburgers is enticing ~~me and my friends~~ my friends and me to try their burgers.

10. My friends want to try ~~they~~ them.

11. ~~Them~~ They aren't being loyal to Bucky's Burgers.

12. I know that Bucky's Burgers still has ~~I~~ me as a loyal customer, though.

Proofreader's Marks

Change text:
~~Her~~ She is a loyal customer.

See all Proofreader's Marks on page ix.

Write It

C. **Answer the questions about where you like to eat. Use subject and object pronouns in your answers.**

13. What restaurant are you a loyal customer of? I am a loyal customer of ______________________________.

14. What food does the restaurant serve? The restaurant serves ______________________________.

15. Who takes you to eat there? ______________________________

16. Why might you change your loyalty? ______________________________.

D. **(17–20) Imagine that you could open your own ice cream stand or burger place. Write at least four sentences to tell how you would attract loyal customers. Use subject and object pronouns.**

____

____

____

____

____

Name ______________________ Date ____________

Edit and Proofread

Capitalize the Names of Groups

- Capitalize each main word in the name of a specific organization, business, or agency.
  Organization: Korean American Coalition
  Business: D'Andrea Italian Market
  Agency: U.S. Census Bureau
- Do not capitalize **on**, **and**, **for**, **of**, or **the** unless they are the first word in the title.
  Council on Foreign Relations
  U.S. Citizenship and Immigration Services

Try It

A. Use proofreader's marks to correct the capitalization error in each sentence.

Proofreader's Marks

Capitalize:
I belong to the cherokee nation.

Do not capitalize:
This Tribe endured the Trail of Tears.

See all Proofreader's Marks on page ix.

1. Michael is a volunteer for the Association On American Indian Affairs.
2. The association helps native tribes gain recognition by the United States government.
3. Members of a recognized tribe can receive services through the Bureau Of Indian Affairs.
4. The Mashpee Wampanoag Tribal council was recently recognized.
5. This was the tribe that befriended the pilgrims when they arrived in 1620.

B. Answer each question. Be sure to capitalize the names of groups correctly.

6. What cultural organizations does your school have?

____

7. What clubs or organizations at your school do you belong to?

____

Name ______________________ Date ______________

Use Semicolons Correctly

- Use a **semicolon** to join two complete sentences that are closely related. Do not capitalize the first word after the semicolon unless it's a proper noun.

  Hector is Guatemalan; however, he wasn't born in Guatemala.

  Pedro, his father, came to the United States in 1991; Carmen, his mother, came in 1992.

- Use a semicolon to combine two sentences, or use a connecting word like **however** or **therefore**. Place a **semicolon** before the connecting word and a **comma** after it.

  Incorrect: Hector was born in 1993, his brother was born in 1995.

  Correct: Hector was born in 1993; his brother was born in 1995.

  Incorrect: Both boys speak English at school however they speak Spanish at home.

  Correct: Both boys speak English at school; **however**, they speak Spanish at home.

Try It

Proofreader's Marks

Add a semicolon:

I am Lithuanian;my best friend is Romanian.

A. Edit each sentence. Add a semicolon in the correct place. Add a comma where needed.

8. Most of the people in Guatemala have some Spanish ancestry;however,they also have Mayan ancestry.

9. Semana Santa is Guatemala's biggest festival;it is a combination of both Catholic and Mayan traditions.

10. Artists prepare elaborate sawdust rugs to line the streets; they are trampled on during the procession that follows.

B. **(11–12) Write a short paragraph about a cultural festival or celebration that you have been to or read about. Use at least two semicolons in your paragraph. Use *however* or *therefore* in one of your sentences. Remember to put a comma after the connecting word.**

____

____

Name ______________________ Date ____________

Choose Active or Passive Voice

- A verb is in the active voice if the subject of the sentence does, or performs, the action. Most sentences are in the active voice.

  Bill Withers **wrote** "Lean on Me."
  Mick Jagger **has recorded** songs by Bill Withers.

- A verb is in the passive voice if the subject receives the action. A verb in the passive voice has a form of the verb **be** and a form of the main verb.

  The song "Use Me" **was written by** Bill Withers.
  "Use Me" **was recorded** recently by the cast of Glee.

- Use **active voice** when you want to emphasize the subject. Use **passive voice** (1) when you want less emphasis on the subject; (2) when you don't know who the doer is; (3) when you don't want to mention the doer or place blame.

  "Lean on Me" **was recorded** by Michael Bolton. (We know the doer.)
  "Down By the River" **was written** long ago. (We don't know the doer.)
  Some songs **are ruined**. (We don't want to name the singer.)

Try It

A. Read each sentence. Decide whether it should be written in the active or passive voice. If it should be in the active voice, rewrite the sentence.

13. The annual Multicultural Festival was held by our school on Friday night.
Our school held the annual Multicultural Festival on Friday night.

14. Dances and music from all over the word were performed by the students.
Students performed dances and music from all over the world.

15. A traditional Indian folk dance was performed by Devi and Sahira.
Devi and Sahira performed a traditional Indian folk dance.

16. Their dance was first performed centuries ago in India.
no changes needed

B. (17–18) Write two sentences about a type of music you like. Use active voice in the first sentence. Use passive voice to tell about music for which you don't know the origin.

Name ______________________ Date ______________

✓ Use Subject Pronouns Correctly

- Use a **subject pronoun** to refer back to a noun in the subject of a sentence.

  Ralph is Filipino. He speaks English and Filipino.
  noun — pronoun

  Ming is Chinese. She speaks English and Mandarin.
  noun — pronoun

- Use subject pronouns to make your writing less repetitive.

  Ralph and Ming are each fluent in two languages. **They** are also learning Spanish.

Subject Pronouns	
Singular	**Plural**
I	we
you	you
he, she, it	they

Try It

A. Add a subject pronoun to complete each pair of sentences.

19. My friend Nastasiya celebrates her Ukrainian heritage. ___She___ belongs to a Ukrainian folk dance group.

20. The members of the group perform at various weddings and festivals. ___They___ dress in colorful costumes.

21. I went to see Nastasiya dance at a banquet. ___It___ was held at the American Legion Hall.

22. Nastasiya danced with a partner. ___They___ danced the hopak.

23. The hopak is a fast dance. ___It___ has been around since the beginning of the sixteenth century.

24. The dance includes many acrobatic jumps. ___They___ require strong legs and good balance.

Name ______________________ Date ____________

46 How Do I Show Possession?

One Way Is to Use a Possessive Noun.

Use a **possessive noun** to show that someone owns, or possesses, something. Add **'s** if the possessive noun names one owner.

My mother left a note for us. My **mother's** note was on the refrigerator.

My brother writes notes on our calendar. My **brother's** notes help us keep up with his schedule.

My older sister is busy, too. My **sister's** schedule is on the bulletin board in the kitchen.

A possessive noun can name more than one owner. Follow these rules:

1. Add only an apostrophe if the plural noun ends in **-s**.

   I read my **sisters'** schedules to find them today.

2. Add **'s** if the plural noun does not end in **-s**.

   Children's schedules can be very busy!

Try It

A. Rewrite each sentence about a family's communication. Turn the underlined words into a possessive noun.

1. The top priority of my family is keeping in touch. My family's top priority is keeping in touch.
2. The cell phone number of each family member is posted on the bulletin board. Each family member's cell phone number is posted on the bulletin board.
3. A note from my parents on the counter said they will be home later than usual. My parents' note on the counter said they will be home later than usual.
4. Messages from my brother are usually taped to the refrigerator. My brother's messages are usually taped to the refrigerator.

B. **(5–9) Complete each sentence with the possessive form of the noun in parentheses.**

Text messages and e-mail are my friends' **(friends)** favorite methods of communication. Paul's **(Paul)** messages are short and funny. Olya's **(Olya)** messages are longer and full of questions. In Oscar's **(Oscar)** opinion, e-mail is the best way to send messages. I like getting all my friends' **(friends)** notes, whether via e-mail or text message.

Write It

C. **Answer the questions about communication. Use possessive nouns in your responses.**

10. In what ways does your family communicate with you? ____________________

11. What are ways your friends communicate with you? ____________________

D. **(12–15) Write at least four more sentences about your communication with family and friends. Use possessive nouns.**

____

____

____

____

Edit It

E. **(16–20) Edit the journal entry. Fix the five mistakes with possessives.**

May 15

My uncle's house is right next door. My aunts' house is far away, beside my grandparents house. My relatives letters keep us in touch. My familys distance does not stop us from communicating. My mothers' wish is that we stay in close contact.

Proofreader's Marks

Add an apostrophe:

My fathers note said he would be back in five minutes.

Transpose:

My sisters' cell phone is off.

See all Proofreader's Marks on page ix.

Name ______________________ Date ____________

47 What's a Possessive Adjective?

It's an Ownership Word.

- Use a **possessive adjective** to tell who has or owns something. Put the possessive adjective before the **noun**.

  My uncle talks about the past. **His children** love to listen.

  My uncle tells stories about my grandmother. **Her family** was very interesting.

  My uncle and grandmother laugh together. **Their memories** make them smile.

- Match the possessive adjective to the **noun** or **pronoun** that it goes with.

  1. **Uncle Raul** (noun) is talking. **His** brother is laughing.
  2. **They** (pronoun) listen closely. **Their** eyes are focused on Uncle Raul.

Subject Pronoun	Possessive Adjective
I	my
you	your
he	his
she	her
it	its
we	our
they	their

Try It

A. Complete each sentence about a storyteller. Write the correct possessive adjective.

1. My uncle talks about his childhood. We love to hear ___his___ (**him / his**) stories.
2. Sarah knows many of the stories. ___Her___ (**She / Her**) father tells them often.
3. My uncle remembers when my parents got married. ___Their___ (**They / Their**) wedding was beautiful.
4. My family asks my uncle questions about the past. ___Our___ (**We / Our**) family history is important to us.
5. I don't want our visit to end. ___My___ (**I / My**) favorite family visits are those I spend talking, laughing, and listening to stories about my loved ones.

B. (6–11) Complete the sentences about a person who communicates through stories. Use **my**, **his**, **her**, **its**, **our**, and **their**.

I have friends who tell stories. We talk between ___our___ classes at school. ___My___ friend Oleg tells stories about everything. To share details about ___his___ day, he tells a story. ___Its___ details might include where, when, why, or how something happened. His sister Katya also tells stories to describe activities, like a trip to the mall or how she found ___her___ great new outfit. Oleg and Katya are interesting. ___Their___ stories help me imagine details about their experiences.

Write It

C. **Answer the questions about communicating through stories. Use possessive adjectives.**

12. Who do you know who likes to communicate through stories? ____________________

____

13. How do you use storytelling in your communication with others? ____________________

____

14. What types of details do you and your friends or family share through stories? __________

____

15. How is storytelling different from just sharing facts? ____________________

____

16. Why do you think some people tend to tell stories, while others do not? __________

____

D. (17–20) **Write at least four sentences that tell more about storytelling as a way to communicate. Use possessive adjectives.**

____

____

____

____

____

Name ______________________ Date ____________

48 What Are the Possessive Pronouns?

Mine, *Yours*, *His*, *Hers*, *Ours*, and *Theirs*

Possessive Adjectives	my	your	her	his	our	their
Possessive Pronouns	mine	yours	hers	his	ours	theirs

Possessive adjectives are used before a **noun**.

Possessive pronouns stand alone.

This is **my** photograph.	This photograph is **mine**.
Your song is beautiful.	The song is **yours**.
This photo album is full of **our** pictures.	The pictures are **ours**.
Her letter is sealed with a stamp.	The letter is **hers**.
They sell sculptures at **their** art gallery.	The art gallery is **theirs**.

Try It

A. Write the possessive pronoun that corresponds to the underlined words. Then rewrite each sentence with the possessive pronoun.

1. We wrote this song about friendship. It is <u>our song</u>. ours; It is ours.

2. This letter is <u>her letter</u>. hers; This letter is hers.

3. The letter is from her father. The words are <u>his words</u>. his; The words are his.

4. The pictures in the photo album are <u>their pictures</u>. theirs; The pictures in the photo album are theirs.

5. They gave the photo album to me. It is <u>my photo album</u>. mine; It is mine.

B. **Form sentence pairs about creative ways to communicate. Draw a line from the first sentence to the one that contains the correct possessive pronoun.**

6. My friend wrote me a letter.	It is hers.
7. I wrote a song to thank my brother.	It is theirs.
8. The author wrote a poem for his daughter.	It is his.
9. Our art teacher painted a picture for us to hang in our class.	It is mine.
10. We gave my grandparents a photo album with pictures we took throughout the year.	It is ours.

Write It

C. **Answer the questions about creative ways of communicating. Use possessive pronouns.**

11. What creative forms of communication have you received from family and friends?

____

12. What creative means of communication have you used with loved ones? ______________

13. What traits make communication through a song or poem special? ______________

14. Describe a song, poem, or photograph you received and cherish. Tell about the person who gave it to you. ______________________________

15. What have you learned about others through photographs, pictures, songs, or poems that you might not have learned through a conversation? ______________

D. **(16–20) Write at least five additional sentences about creative forms of communication you have shared with others. Use possessive pronouns.**

____

____

____

____

____

____

Name ______________________ Date ____________

49 What's a Reflexive Pronoun?

It's a Word for the Same Person.

- Use a **reflexive pronoun** to talk about the same person or thing twice in a sentence. Reflexive pronouns end in -**self** or -**selves**.

  I listen to **myself** as I speak.

  My sister repeats **herself**.

  My friends repeat **themselves**.

Reflexive Pronouns	
Singular	**Plural**
myself	ourselves
yourself	yourselves
himself, herself, itself	themselves

- Avoid these common mistakes with reflexive pronouns.

  1. People repeat ~~theirselves~~ themselves to be understood.
  2. Mike says that sometimes he cannot even understand ~~hisself~~ himself.

Try It

A. Complete the sentences with the correct reflexive pronoun.

1. I read my letters to ____myself____ (myself / ourself) before I send them.
2. People sometimes repeat ____themselves____ (theirself / themselves) to be clear.
3. My mother repeats ____herself____ (herself / himself) to be sure we understand her.
4. In drama class, we watch ____ourselves____ (ourself / ourselves) act on video.

B. (5–8) Complete the sentences. Use themselves, ourselves, herself, and himself.

My classmates and I were afraid to speak in front of the class. We surprised ____ourselves____! We learned how people prepare ____themselves____ to speak for an audience. My teacher practices while looking at ____himself____ in the mirror. My mother visualizes ____herself____ speaking to be sure her message is clear.

Write It

C. Answer the questions about communicating clearly. Use reflexive pronouns.

9. When might a person practice speaking to himself or herself before speaking to others?

____

10. When might people need to repeat themselves to communicate more clearly? __________

____

D. (11–15) Write at least five sentences that describe communicating clearly. Use reflexive pronouns.

____

____

____

____

____

Edit It

E. (16–20) Edit the paragraph. Fix the five mistakes with reflexive pronouns.

Do people sometimes ask you to repeat yourself? Do you sometimes have trouble expressing ~~youself~~ yourself clearly? Many people have trouble expressing ~~theirselves~~ themselves. I have learned ways to help ~~mineself~~ myself communicate more clearly. My father repeats himself if people look confused. He says, "When we explain ~~ourself~~ ourselves a second time, we should try to use different words to clarify our thoughts." A friend of mine speaks quietly. When she repeats ~~himself~~ herself more loudly, people usually understand her.

Proofreader's Marks

Change text:

We need to listen to ~~ourself~~ ourselves speak!

See all Proofreader's Marks on page ix.

Name ______________________ Date ______________

50 Show Possession

Remember: Use possessive words to show that someone owns something. A possessive adjective comes before a noun. A possessive pronoun stands alone.

Possessive Adjectives	my	your	his	her	its	our	your	their
Possessive Pronouns	mine	yours	his	hers		ours	yours	theirs

Try It

A. **Complete each sentence about conversations. Write the correct possessive adjectives and possessive pronouns.**

1. My classmates have many conversations. ___Their___ (**Their / Theirs**) conversations reveal opinions and character traits.

2. A conversation can occur between two or more people. ___Its___ (**Its / His**) purpose is communicating thoughts and ideas.

3. One boy in class has a habit of speaking but not listening. This habit is ___his___ (**his / hers**).

4. In class discussions, the teacher reminds us to speak and listen. Our teacher wants us to communicate ___our___ (**our / ours**) ideas effectively.

B. **Complete each sentence. Use a possessive adjective or a possessive pronoun.**

5. My siblings do not communicate well. ___Their___ chats become arguments.

6. Sometimes I debate with my friends. I listen closely and respond, based on the thoughts of my friends. This technique is ___mine___.

7. My aunt understands people. ___Her___ mind is open to different perspectives.

8. People love to talk to my uncle. ___His___ sense of humor makes us all laugh.

Write It

C. **Answer the questions about good conversations. Use possessive adjectives and possessive pronouns.**

9. What people do you like having conversations with? I like having conversations with people who are ______________________________.

10. What traits make it appealing to speak with them? ______________________________

____

11. What actions of good listeners show that they listen? ______________________________

____

D. **(12–15) Write at least four more sentences to describe conversations. Use possessive adjectives and possessive pronouns.**

____

____

____

____

____

Edit It

E. **(16–20) Edit the letter. Fix the five mistakes with possessives.**

Dear Mr. Warren,

There is one class I look forward to every day in school. It's yours! In ~~yours~~ your class, the students listen closely. ~~Ours~~ Our eyes are always focused on you. This is because you recognize our skills and help us use them to learn. Also, ~~yours~~ your lessons are interesting. You bring history to life. You teach us ~~it~~ its value in modern society. Thank you for such a great class.

Your student,

Lydia

Proofreader's Marks

Add text:

The funniest joke was. (yours)

Delete:

Hers stories are the best.

See all Proofreader's Marks on page ix.

Name ____________________ Date ____________

51 What Kinds of Things Do Prepositions Show?

Location, Direction, Time, and Origin

Prepositions That Show Location: in, on top of, on, at, over, under, above, below, next to, beside, in front of, in back of, behind

- Use a preposition of **location** to tell where something is.

  On the bus, we talked about our plans.

Prepositions That Show Direction: up, down, through, across, into, to

- Use a preposition of **direction** to tell where something is going.

  We took the bus **to** the movies.

Prepositions That Show Time: after, until, before, during

- Use a preposition of time to tell **when** something happens.

  After the bus ride, we ate lunch.

Preposition That Shows Origin: from

- Use a preposition of **origin** to tell where someone is from.

  We met someone on the bus who is **from** England.

Try It

A. **Complete each sentence about communicating at a concert. Use a correct preposition.** Possible responses:

1. We went to a concert ___across___ town.
2. ___During___ the concert, my friend wanted to borrow my camera.
3. She was right ___next to___ me but had to yell loudly.
4. I was finally able to hear her. I placed my camera ___in___ her hands.
5. She took several great photographs ___after___ the concert.

B. **Complete each sentence. Write the correct preposition. Then tell whether the preposition shows location, direction, time, or origin.**

6. We were in a hurry to get through; direction the line.
through / until

7. We were standing behind; location a lady with a small number of groceries.
at / behind

8. She is our neighbor. She is from; origin Guatemala.
from / before

Write It

C. **Answer the questions about challenges in communicating in daily situations. Use prepositions of location, direction, time, and origin.**

9. In which locations can people have difficulty hearing or seeing each other? ____________

____

10. What can they do to get their ideas across to each other? ____________

D. **(11–14) Write at least four more sentences about challenges in communicating in daily situations. Use prepositions of location, direction, time, and origin.**

____

____

____

____

Edit It

E. **(15–20) Edit the article. Fix the six mistakes in prepositions.**

It is difficult to communicate during a movie. It is quiet enough to talk to the person sitting next ~~of~~ to you. But you can't talk too often or too loudly during a movie. Other people in front of you and in back of you can't hear the movie with you talking. It is best to wait until the movie is over to discuss it. You can go to a coffee shop ~~during~~ after the movie is over and talk about it there.

Proofreader's Marks

Add text:

I put my ticket in my pocket.

Change text:

I try not to talk ~~from~~ during a movie.

See all Proofreader's Marks on page ix.

Name ______________________ Date ____________

52 How Do You Recognize a Prepositional Phrase?

Look for the Preposition.

- A **phrase** is a group of related words. A **prepositional phrase** begins with a preposition and ends with a noun or pronoun. Use prepositional phrases to add information to your sentences.

  We tried to talk **after class**, but we had to hurry.
  (noun)

  We looked **at our watches** every minute.
  (noun)

- The **noun** or **pronoun** at the end of a prepositional phrase is called the **object of the preposition**.

Try It

A. Read each sentence about teens communicating. Complete the prepositional phrase with an object. Possible responses:

1. I needed to tell Sara about the play.
2. I saw her in the hall after class.
3. I asked her to meet me after school for directions to the theater.
4. We had to hurry because class was going to start in five minutes.
5. She went toward her class and I went in the opposite direction.
6. I wasn't sure Sara understood me until we met after school.

B. Complete each sentence with a prepositional phrase from the box.

after a few seconds	at a restaurant	on my cell phone

7. My friends planned to meet at a restaurant.
8. Paul called me on my cell phone to tell me where to go and when.
9. I heard Paul speaking; however, after a few seconds, his voice started to fade.

Write It

C. Answer the questions below about communicating. Use prepositional phrases.

10. What are some situations in school that present problems when people want to communicate? ______________________________

11. What results have you had when you tried to overcome obstacles in communication?

____

12. What are alternative ways of communicating in these situations? ______________________________

____

D. (13–15) **Write at least three sentences about challenges and problems in communicating with other teens. Use prepositional phrases.**

____

____

____

____

Edit It

E. (16–20) **Edit the letter. Fix the five mistakes in prepositional phrases.**

Dear Brandon,

Your sister and I rode the bus together yesterday after class. While I was on the bus, I tried to draw a map from your house to mine. The ride was bumpy, so I made messy errors ~~during~~ on the map. I ran out of time before your sister had to get off at her stop. I folded the map and gave it ~~for~~ to your sister. Did she pass it along ~~of~~ to you? If you cannot understand it, please call me ~~below~~ before tomorrow so I can explain the directions before you leave.

Your friend,

Mica

Proofreader's Marks

Change text:

It is hard to write ~~at~~ on a bus.

See all Proofreader's Marks on page ix.

Name ________________________________ Date ________________

53 Can I Use a Pronoun After a Preposition?

Yes, Use an Object Pronoun.

- Use an **object pronoun** after a **preposition**.

  At the game, friends shout to **us**.

  It is sometimes hard to pay attention to **them**.

Object Pronouns	
Singular	**Plural**
me	us
you	you
him, her, it	them

Try It

A. (1–5) **Complete the sentences about communicating during a sporting event. Use the correct object pronoun.**

Communicating on the field is easy. I give Cara a signal, and she passes the ball to ___me___. If she wants me to toss the ball to ___her___, she nods. Teammates use different signals that show what we need to do for ___them___. The other team does not know our signals. This makes the signals even more useful to ___us___. Our coach teaches us about communication. He says every team benefits from ___it___.

B. **Complete the sentences about communication during a volleyball game. Use me, them, you, us, and her.**

6. I communicate with teammates during volleyball games. I whisper to ___them___.

7. My teammates also communicate with ___me___ during games.

8. Look for signals. If we point to ___you___, that means you should spike the ball.

9. Stand in position before Cindy serves. This is a signal for ___her___ that we are ready.

10. When we play games, our schoolmates yell cheers for ___us___ from the bleachers.

Write It

C. **Answer the questions about communicating during sporting events. Use object pronouns after prepositions.**

11. What are ways team members communicate with each other during games? ________________

____

12. Why is it important to have signals that each player understands? ________________

____

13. How can players be sure teammates understood the signals sent to them? ________________

____

D. **(14–15) Write at least two more sentences about communicating during games or events. Use object pronouns after prepositions.**

____

____

____

Edit It

E. **(16–20) Edit the article. Fix the five mistakes in pronouns after prepositions.**

Many signals are used between players during a baseball game. The signals are useful to them. Spectators make signals to ~~they~~ them through cheering or booing. On our team, we use many signals. Our coaches make signals for ~~we~~ us using hand motions and by mouthing words. People give signals to the pitcher. The catcher makes signs to ~~you~~ him that show him how to pitch the ball. The batter can't see the signal. He has to bat without ~~me~~ it and has little time to react when the ball races toward ~~he~~ him.

Proofreader's Marks

Change text:

The signals are useful to ~~they~~ them.

See all Proofreader's Marks on page ix.

Name ______________________ Date ______________

54 In a Prepositional Phrase, Where Does the Pronoun Go?

It Goes Last.

- A **prepositional phrase** starts with a preposition and ends with a noun or pronoun. Sometimes, it ends with both. Put the pronoun last.

  Nadja is Farwa's sister. Sometimes communication **between Farwa and her** is confusing.

  Farwa cannot understand what Nadja is trying to say **to her**.

- You can put a prepositional phrase at the start of the sentence to emphasize your idea.

  For the sisters and me, there are many activities to choose from today.

- Avoid these common mistakes in a prepositional phrase:

  1. Use **me,** not **I**:

  Farwa's games are fun for Nadja and ~~I~~ me.

  2. Put **me** last:

  Farwa has many activities planned for ~~me and Nadja~~ Nadja and me today.

Try It

A. (1–7) **Complete each sentence about communication between siblings. Choose the correct object pronoun from the choices in parentheses.**

Today Nadja is going to the park with her sister. It should be a good day for Nadja and ____her____. **(she / her)** Nadja and Farwa invited me to go with them. It will be exciting for them and ____me____. **(I / me)** Farwa hoped the games would be fun for her and ____us____. **(we / us)** Once Nadja told Farwa that the games were not fun for ____her____ **(she / her)** and me. Farwa got upset. She thought her ideas were boring for Nadja and ____me____. **(I / me)** I explained that the games were a lot of fun. I hugged Nadja and ____her____. **(she / her)** I am glad we made up. Farwa and Nadja saw their parents calling for ____them____ **(they / them)** and me. It was time to go.

B. Complete the sentences by drawing a line to the correct prepositional phrase.

8. Joseph has many friends. His little brother Henry likes to play
9. Sometimes Henry and Joseph make the rules of a game. Henry tells everyone to listen
10. Today they invited me to come over with friends. I knew it would be fun
11. Henry said that Joseph was ignoring him by talking to friends. Joseph talked
12. We explained to Henry that we were happy he came along. It was a relief

for them and me.

to Henry and them.

with Joseph and them.

to him and us.

to Joseph and him.

Write It

C. Answer the questions about communication. Use prepositional phrases and pronouns.

13. What are common situations in which family members misunderstand each other?

____

14. Share an example of a time a family member was hurt due to misunderstanding words or signals. ______________________________

15. Share an example of a time that you misunderstood words or signals from a family member. ______________________________

16. What are ways to notice when someone has misunderstood, and to explain the truth to him or her? ______________________________

D. (17–20) Write at least four sentences that tell more about situations when friends and family members miscommunicate. Use prepositional phrases that include pronouns.

____

____

____

____

Name ______________________ Date ____________

55 Use Pronouns in Prepositional Phrases

Remember: You can use prepositions to add details to your sentences. If you need a pronoun in a prepositional phrase, use an object pronoun.

Sentences with Prepositional Phrases

- Sometimes I confuse new acquaintances when I am **around them**.
- I am very shy. This morning, a girl thought I didn't want to talk **to her**.
- I like meeting girls. But it is hard to be outgoing **with them**.
- My friends and I are shy. It is easier **for them and me** to be outgoing when we are together.

Object Pronouns	
Singular	**Plural**
me	us
you	you
him, her, it	them

Try It

A. Read the conversation between two friends. Add an object pronoun to complete each prepositional phrase.

1. "Paula, I met a new friend named Liliana. I gave a party invitation to ___her___.

2. But she smiled and walked away. She must not want to spend time with ___me___."

3. "Kim, Liliana told me that she was happy that you invited her. She asked me if she should bring snacks or games for ___us___ when she comes."

4. "That's great, Paula. It will be fun for Liliana and ___us___.

5. Also, you know both Liliana and ___me___. With you there, we can all probably understand one another better."

B. **(6–10) Complete the paragraph about miscommunication with the correct object pronouns from the box.**

he	him	I	me	them	they	us	we

Possible responses:

I planned to meet Niko and a few other friends at the movies on Saturday. I thought it would be fun for ___them___ and ___me___. I looked for ___them___ in front of the theater at 5 p.m. Niko and I noticed that Victor wasn't there. At first, it worried ___him___ and me, but we figured Victor decided not to come. After the movie ended, Victor called me to ask where he should park. Victor thought I said to meet at 8 p.m. Luckily, he wasn't angry with Niko and ___us___.

Write It

C. **Answer the questions about a miscommunication that you resolved with friends or relatives. Use prepositional phrases and object pronouns.**

11. When have you miscommunicated with a friend or relative? ______________________

12. How did he or she react to the situation? ______________________

13. How did you and your friend or relative resolve the miscommunication? ______________________

____

14. What did you learn about communicating with others from the situation? ______________________

____

15. What will you do differently the next time you are in a similar situation? ______________________

____

D. **(16–20) Write at least five more sentences about a miscommunication that you resolved with friends or relatives. Use prepositional phrases and object pronouns.**

____

____

____

____

____

____

Name ____________________ Date ____________

56 When Do You Use an Indefinite Pronoun?

When You Can't Be Specific

- When you are not talking about a specific person or thing, you can use an **indefinite pronoun**.

  Everything is ready for our trip.

- Some indefinite pronouns are always singular, so they need a **singular verb** that ends in **-s**.

  Nothing feel**s** nicer than visiting family.

Singular Indefinite Pronouns			
another	each	everything	nothing
anybody	either	neither	somebody
anyone	everybody	nobody	someone
anything	everyone	no one	something

Try It

A. Complete each sentence. Choose the correct verb to go with the indefinite pronoun.

1. Nobody __believes__ (believe / believes) that most of my family lives in Argentina.

2. Everyone in my family here __understands__ (understand / understands) English.

3. When someone __speaks__ (speak / speaks) Spanish, we understand him or her perfectly.

B. (4–7) Complete each sentence about a student's first day at school. Use someone, everyone, neither, no one, or something. Possible responses:

It is my first day of school. It seems that __everyone__ speaks English well except me. __No one__ wants to sit alone in the cafeteria. As I stand in line, __something__ makes me feel better. I hear two girls speaking Mandarin. __Neither__ of them knows me yet, but I will introduce myself.

Write It

C. **Answer the questions about learning a language. Use indefinite pronouns.**

8. Why might someone enjoy learning a new language? ______________________

9. Does each person in your family speak the same language or languages? Explain.

____

10. Can anyone learn a new language? Explain. ______________________

____

D. **(11–15) Write at least five more sentences about learning languages. Use indefinite pronouns.**

____

____

____

____

____

Edit It

E. **(16–20) Edit the journal entry. Fix the five mistakes in indefinite pronouns or verbs.**

November 20

My friend Sasha is from Russia. There, everyone speaks Russian. ^Everybody feels homesick when ^somebody speaks his language on television. No#one in our class speaks Russian fluently except Sasha. Each of his friends ^knows a few words in Russian from Sasha. But ~~anybody~~ ^nobody has the time to learn more.

Proofreader's Marks

Add text:
^Someone talked to me in my language!

Change text:
I didn't know ~~somebody~~ ^anybody.

Add a space:
No#one likes to feel left out.

See all Proofreader's Marks on page ix.

Name ______________________ Date ______________

57 Which Indefinite Pronouns Are Plural?

Both, Few, Many and Several

- Use an **indefinite pronoun** when you are not talking about a specific person or thing.

  Both of my parents know sign language.

  Several of their friends use it as well.

- Some **indefinite pronouns** are always plural, so they need a **plural verb**.

  Many in the world communicate through sign language.

  A **few** of the people we know use international sign language.

Plural Indefinite Pronouns	
both	many
few	several

Try It

A. Complete each sentence about communicating through sign language. Write the correct form of the verb.

1. My parents are deaf. Both of them ___use___ (use / uses) sign language to communicate.

2. Several of their friends ___know___ (know / knows) sign language, too.

3. Many of my hearing relatives ___use___ (use / uses) sign language at our house.

4. A few of these people ___communicate___ (communicate / communicates) with my parents by writing because they do not know sign language.

5. Both of my brothers ___enjoy___ (enjoy / enjoys) using sign language at their jobs as translators.

6. Many of my classmates at school ___take___ (take / takes) the sign language class.

7. Several of us ___hope___ (hope / hopes) to use sign language in future jobs.

B. **Complete the sentences about a sign language class. Use the correct form of the verb in parentheses.**

8. A few of our schoolmates ___use___ sign language to communicate with relatives. **(use)**

9. Several of my friends ___study___ sign language in special classes. We volunteer at a school for children who are deaf. **(study)**

10. Both of my best friends ___know___ sign language and use it to communicate with people in various situations. **(know)**

Write It

C. **Answer the questions about using sign language. Use plural indefinite pronouns.**

11. Have you seen people communicating in sign language? I have seen ____________________

____.

12. In what situations have you seen people communicating in sign language? Explain.

____

13. How is sign language similar to and different from other languages? ____________________

____

14. What are reasons that people learn sign language? ____________________

____

15. Why is knowing sign language useful for people who hear? ____________________

____

D. (16–20) **Write at least five sentences that tell more about communication through sign language. Use plural indefinite pronouns.**

____

____

____

____

____

Name ______________________ Date ____________

58 Which Indefinite Pronouns Are Tricky?

The Ones That Can Be Singular or Plural

- The **indefinite pronouns** in the chart can be either singular or plural.
- The prepositional phrase after the pronoun shows whether the sentence talks about one thing or more than one thing. Use the correct **verb**.

Singular: I volunteer at an animal rescue organization. **Most** of the **organization** loves pets.

Plural: **Most** of the **people** have cats.

Singular: **Some** of my **family** loves dogs

Plural: **Some** of my **relatives** love dogs.

Singular or Plural Indefinite Pronouns	
all	none
any	some
most	

Try It

A. Complete the sentences about communicating with animals. Use the correct verb form.

1. We have a pet cat. None of my friends understand (understand / understands) the cat.
2. All of my family knows (know / knows) how well I understand my cat.
3. My cat gives me hints. Most of the hints are (is / are) clear to me.
4. Some of the world believes (believe / believes) that cats do not have emotions.
5. All of my cat's emotions are (is / are) easy for me to see and hear.
6. My cat is a picky eater. Sometimes none of the food is (is / are) eaten.
7. Any of her favorite foods get (get / gets) gobbled up right away.
8. None of my cat's behavior surprises (surprise / surprises) me.

B. Choose words from each column to write sentences about owning animals.

All	of my classmates	ask me how to train a dog.
Most	of my family	has pets.
None	of my friends	have a dog.
Some	of our neighborhood	understands how to train dogs.

Possible responses:

9. All of our neighborhood has pets.

10. None of my friends have a dog.

11. Some of my family understands how to train dogs.

12. Most of my classmates ask me how to train a dog.

Write It

C. **Answer the questions about people and pets. Use singular or plural indefinite pronouns.**

13. What percentage of people you know can communicate well with animals? ______

______

14. Are most pets you have seen trained well? Explain. ______

______

15. Do most pets you have seen love their owners? Why do you think so? ______

______

D. (16–20) **Write at least five more sentences about understanding animals. Use singular or plural indefinite pronouns.**

______

______

______

______

______

Name ______________________ Date __________

59 What's an "Antecedent"?

It's the Word a Pronoun Refers To.

- A **pronoun** usually refers back to a noun. This noun is called the **antecedent**.

  Artists paint murals on buildings. **They** communicate through these pictures.
  antecedent — pronoun

- A pronoun must **agree** with its antecedent. This means that the pronoun has to go with the noun it refers to.

  Murals are large paintings. **They** can be seen on inside or outside walls.

  Susanna and I love the mural in the cafeteria. **We** think it communicates school spirit!

Try It

A. Rewrite the sentences. Replace the underlined antecedents with pronouns that agree.

1. In the winter, sculptors carve ice sculptures in the park. In the winter, they carve ice sculptures in the park.

2. My family and I go to see the ice sculptures every year. We go to see the ice sculptures every year.

3. Alicia thinks the artist is communicating about daily life through the sculptures. She thinks the artist is communicating about daily life through the sculptures.

B. (4–7) Complete each sentence with a pronoun from the box. Match it to the antecedent.

it	he	she	they

Tonya paints murals for a living. She always communicates a message. Parents ask her to paint murals in children's room. They want to create a fun environment. One man hired her to paint an ad for his company. He wanted people to buy his product. A mural is what the artist makes it. It can be fun, serious, interesting, or persuasive.

Write It

C. **Answer the questions about creative forms of communication. Use antecedents and pronouns in your responses.**

8. What forms of creative expression do you like to use? Why? ______________________

____

9. What forms of creative expression are visible in your school? ______________________

____

10. What messages or emotions do you think these forms communicate? ______________________

____

D. (11–15) **Write at least five sentences that tell more about forms of creative expression. Use pronouns and antecedents.**

____

____

____

____

____

Edit It

E. (16–20) **Edit the article. Fix the five mistakes in pronouns.**

Have you seen the murals on the sidewalk? They are a new form of creative expression. A local artist, Juan Moya, began painting them one year ago. ~~They~~ He now enjoys attention from hundreds of people each day. ~~It~~ They stop to admire his art. His work makes people look at things from a new perspective. ~~We~~ It has a meaning all its own. This is his message. ~~They~~ It is communicated through objects and people that sit upside-down, sideways, or in mid-air in everyday places. My family and I love these murals. ~~He~~ We hope Juan Moya paints more of them.

Proofreader's Marks

Change text:

Tim and I sculpt. ~~They~~ We do it all the time.

See all Proofreader's Marks on page ix.

Name ______________________ Date ____________

60 Use the Correct Pronoun

Remember: When you use a pronoun, be sure it fits correctly into the sentence. Also be sure it goes with the noun it refers to.

- Use a **subject pronoun** in the subject of a sentence. Use an **object pronoun** after the verb or after a preposition.

  Marco uses **gestures**. **He** uses **them** to communicate.

  My **parents** say that **eye contact** is important. **They** say **it** helps people understand each other.

- All **pronouns** must agree with the **noun** they refer to. This noun is called the antecedent.
  1. If the noun names a male, use **he** or **him**.
  2. If the noun names a female, use **she** or **her**.
  3. If the noun names one thing, use **it** or **it**.
  4. If the noun names "more than one," use **they** or **them**.

Try It

A. Complete each sentence about gestures and body language. Write the correct verb or pronoun.

1. None of my friends realize (realize / realizes) that they use gestures or body language.
2. Gina communicates through gestures. She uses them (them / they) without even knowing it.
3. My friend Jeremy uses body language with his arms. He (He / They) crosses them when he is angry.
4. Both of my friends keep (keep / keeps) eye contact with others when they are talking.
5. All of my class keeps (keep / keeps) eye contact with the teacher to show that we are listening.

B. (6–11) Edit the paragraph. Fix the six mistakes.

Communication is not only about spoken language. It is also about body language. Almost everyone ^uses body language. It ~~hold~~ ^holds clues about peoples' feelings. Speakers use body language to show confidence. Most of ~~they~~ ^them ~~makes~~ sure to smile and keep straight posture. Most of our feelings ~~is~~ ^are communicated by words, but some of ~~they~~ ^them are also shown through our actions and expressions.

Proofreader's Marks

Delete:

All of my relatives ~~uses~~ body language.

Change text:

Eva knows me. ~~They~~ ^She knows my gestures.

See all Proofreader's Marks on page ix.

Write It

C. Answer the questions about using gestures and body language in communication. Use pronouns, antecedents, and the correct verb forms.

12. What types of gestures and body language do you use? ______________________

____

13. What gestures communicate positive feelings? ______________________

____

14. What gestures or body language communicate negative feelings? ______________________

____

15. Why do people use gestures and body language? ______________________

____

16. Do you think it is important to pay attention to body language? Why or why not?

____

D. (17–20) Write at least four more sentences about gesturing and using body language. Use pronouns and the correct verb forms.

____

____

____

____

____

Name ______________________ Date ____________

Edit and Proofread

Capitalize the Titles of Publications

- Capitalize all main words in the titles of publications, such as books, magazines, newspapers, and articles.

  Book: *Tele-Revolution*

  Magazine: *Wired*

  Newspaper: *USA Today*

  Article: "They've Got Your Number"

- Do not capitalize articles or prepositions, such as **a**, **an**, **the**, **on**, and **of** unless they are the first word in the title.

  Vintage Telephones of the World

  The New York Times

Try It

Proofreader's Marks

Capitalize:

Joe reads *wireless news*.

Do not capitalize:

Nicole is reading *The Telephone And Its Several Inventors*.

See all Proofreader's Marks on page ix.

A. Fix the capitalization error in each sentence. Use proofreader's marks.

1. I'm looking for a book called *the History of the Telephone*.
2. *PC magazine* has an entertaining article on cell phones.
3. The article is called "Aren't Phones For Talking?"
4. Did you read "Capturing The Camera Phone"?
5. It was in this morning's edition of *the chicago Tribune*.

B. Answer each question. Be sure to capitalize titles correctly.

6. What is the name of your local newspaper?

   ____

7. What is the title of your math book?

   ____

8. What is the title of a magazine article you read recently?

   ____

Name ______________________ Date ______________

Use Parentheses Correctly

Use parentheses to enclose:

- Explanatory information

  The multimedia phone (the latest version of the cell phone) is a popular item.

- The source of factual information. The period goes *after* the closing parenthesis.

  Forty-two percent of people aged 18 to 24 said it was important to own a cell phone with a camera (comScore Networks).

- The source of a quotation. The end quotation mark goes *before* the source in parentheses.

  "Manufacturers want to sell expensive multimedia phones" (Segan).

Try It

A. (9–12) Edit the report. Fix four errors with parentheses. Use proofreader's marks.

Today's cell phones let you do more than just talk. You can figure out your location, shoot a small documentary, and become an amateur photographer with this device that's small enough to fit in your pocket. Soon you may be able to do even more. "New technologies and concepts are coming at us like seagulls swooping after a dropped potato chip" (Maney 8). Cell phones have begun to take on functions of the PDA and the personal computer. For instance, many phones now allow you to download, store, and play music; others allow you to e-mail documents. (Press 17) These phones (also known as smartphones) are on the way to becoming "a remote control for your life" (Press 15)."

Proofreader's Marks

Add parentheses:

The first cell phone weighed two pounds (Press 13).

Add quotation marks:

"I forgot my cell phone!" she exclaimed.

Add a period:

He found his cell phone.

Delete:

It it was in the cafeteria.

Name ______________________ Date ______________

Place Modifiers Correctly

Modifiers are words, phrases, or clauses that modify, or describe, other words in a sentence.

- To avoid **misplaced modifiers**, put modifiers as close as possible to the words they describe.

  Unclear: Courtney bought a cell phone at the store **with a camera**.
  misplaced modifier

  Ask yourself: What has a camera? The cell phone or the store?

  Clear: Courtney bought a cell phone **with a camera** at the store.
  modifier

  Now it is clear that the cell phone has a camera.

- To avoid a **dangling modifier**, make sure the modifier has a word or group of words to modify. Dangling modifiers usually come at the beginning of the sentence and often start with a verb ending in **-ing**.

  Unclear: While walking home, her new phone rang.
  dangling modifier

  Ask yourself: Who or what was walking home? The new phone?

  Clear: While Peggy was walking home, her new phone rang.
  modifier

  Now it is clear that Peggy was the one walking home.

Try It

A. Rewrite each sentence. Correct the underlined modifier. Possible responses:

13. Courtney's phone had been stolen **while on a field trip**.
While she was on a field trip, Courtney's phone had been stolen.

14. **While searching**, the phone rang.
While she was searching, the phone rang.

15. **Ringing under an exhibit**, she found her phone.
She found her phone ringing under an exhibit.

Name ________________________________ Date ________________

Make Pronouns Agree with Their Antecedents

- A **pronoun** usually refers back to a noun. This noun is called the **antecedent**.

  Where is **my cell phone**? Isn't **it** in your backpack?

  antecedent — pronoun

- A pronoun must agree with its antecedent. It must match the noun it refers to in both gender (male or female) and number (singular or plural).

  Antonio still can't find his cell phone. **He** has looked everywhere.

  Ask **Madeline and Lucy**. **They** were using a cell phone earlier this afternoon.

Try It

A. **(16–18) Complete the story by adding the correct pronouns. Draw an arrow from each pronoun to its antecedent.**

Alexander Graham Bell came up with the idea of the telephone, but ___he___ was not alone. Elisha Gray was another scientist who worked on ___it___. Bell filed a patent for the telephone just hours before Gray did. Gray decided to sue Bell over the rights to the invention. The two men fought in court for many years. ___They___ never reached an agreement, though the court named Bell as the inventor.

B. **(19–20) Edit the excerpt from a report. Fix the two mistakes in pronouns. Use proofreader's marks.**

Guglielmo Marconi and Nikola Tesla worked separately on wireless communication. ~~He~~ They both claimed to be the inventor of the radio. Marconi developed a working transmitter and receiver, but he used Tesla's research. Marconi patented the invention; however, Tesla claimed ~~she~~ it was his. Eventually, the U.S. Patent Office agreed and declared that he was the true inventor.

Proofreader's Marks

Change text:
That phone is broken. ~~It~~ It doesn't work.

Name ______________________________ Date ______________

61 What Are Adjectives?

They Are Describing Words.

- You can describe people, places, or things with **adjectives**. They answer the question: What is it like?
- Use adjectives to describe:
  1. how something looks: **charming, crowded, dusty, empty, elegant, tall**
  2. how something sounds: **chirping, humming, loud, quiet**
  3. how something feels, tastes, or smells: **rough, bumpy, sweet, fragrant**
  4. a person's mood: **anxious, cheery, friendly, frustrated**
- Adjectives help the reader visualize what you are writing about.

  The **crowded** streets are filled with **buzzing** traffic.

  The **dusty** road leads to a **sunny** park.

Try It

A. Complete each sentence with an adjective from the box. Possible responses:

lively	modern	peaceful	simple	sleepy	spicy	towering	vibrant

1. Lukas likes to walk down the streets of the ___sleepy___ town.
2. Victoria admires the ___modern___ buildings in the city.
3. Lukas prefers the ___towering___ trees that line Main Street.
4. She eats ___spicy___ food from the sidewalk vendors.
5. He likes the ___simple___ menu at the corner diner.
6. She goes to street festivals to listen to ___lively___ music.
7. Lukas likes listening to the ___peaceful___ chirping of the birds in the park.
8. Victoria prefers the ___vibrant___ energy of the big city.

B. **Now think of your own adjectives to help the reader visualize how life is different in a big city and a small town. Write the new sentences on the lines.** Possible responses:

9. Lukas gives a wave to everyone he meets on his walk.
Lukas gives a friendly wave to everyone he meets on his walk.

10. Victoria takes the subway to visit the museum.
Victoria takes the crowded subway to visit the museum.

11. The building has exhibits.
The huge building has interesting exhibits.

12. Lukas meets his friend for lunch in the park.
Lukas meets his friend for lunch in the shady park.

Write It

C. **Answer the questions about the differences between small town and city life. Use adjectives.**

13. What do you find in cities? Cities have ______________________________

______________________________.

14. Describe the sounds or sights of a small town. A small town has ______________________________

______________________________.

15. What is the biggest difference between a city and a small town? A city has ______________

______________ and a small town has ______________________________.

D. **(16–20) Write at least five sentences that describe a big city or a small town. Use adjectives in your sentences.**

____

____

____

____

____

____

Name ______________________ Date ____________

62 Where Do Adjectives Appear in a Sentence?

Usually Before the Noun

- Often the **adjective** comes before the **noun** you are describing.
  Bryan rides his **mountain bike** on the **bumpy path**.
  He speeds along in the **cool breeze**.
- If two adjectives both describe the noun, separate them with a comma (,).
  Dennis prefers to draw **huge, colorful paintings**.
  He stays indoors in his **bright, airy room**.

Try It

A. Add adjectives to complete each sentence about two people with different preferences.

Possible responses:

1. Bryan uses ___heavy___ weights to build his muscles.
2. Dennis sets out his paints in the ___brilliant___ sunlight.
3. Most mornings, Bryan completes ___intense___ workouts.
4. Dennis sketches in a ___quiet___ studio.

B. Put the words in the right order and write the sentences. Punctuate your sentences correctly.

5. enjoys / Bryan / fruits and vegetables / fresh Bryan enjoys fresh fruits and vegetables.
6. Dennis / likes / desserts / sweet / to eat Dennis likes to eat sweet desserts.
7. gear / buys / athletic / Bryan / to wear / to the gym Bryan buys athletic gear to wear to the gym.
8. boots / jeans / leather / Dennis / wears / and / blue Dennis wears blue jeans and leather boots.
9. like / Bryan and Dennis / things / different Bryan and Dennis like different things.

Write It

C. **You have two friends who have very different interests. What makes them different? Use adjectives to describe them.**

10. What activities do your two friends enjoy? _______________ likes _______________ and _______________ likes _______________.

11. How are your two friends different? _______________

____

12. Describe one interest that you share with your friends. _______________

____

D. (13–15) **Write at least three sentences that compare two of your friends with different interests. Use adjectives correctly.**

____

____

____

____

Edit It

E. (16–20) **Edit the letter. Add four adjectives and one comma.**

Dear Aunt Helena,

I am riding on the challenging bike path every day. You taught me how to go around the ^tight turns. I am preparing for the long^, difficult race on Saturday. The 5K race is an ^intense competition. With so much riding, I have ^strong legs. I also eat ^healthy foods to prepare for the race.

See you soon,

Bryan

Proofreader's Marks

Add text:

Dennis uses ^colorful paints, too.

Add a comma:

He likes his soft^, comfortable chair.

See all Proofreader's Marks on page ix.

Name ______________________ Date ____________

63 How Do You Use a Predicate Adjective?

After a Form of the Verb *Be*

- Most of the time, **adjectives** come before **nouns**.
  Juan puts his money in a **safe place**. He has a **cautious nature**.
- But if your verb is a form of **be**, you can put the adjective after the verb. The forms of **be** are **am**, **is**, **are**, **was**, and **were**.
  Juan is **careful** with his money. His **spending** is **controlled**.
- If you use two predicate adjectives, join them with **and**, **but**, or **or**.
  Ivan is **outgoing** and **generous**. His **hobbies** are **exciting** but **expensive**.
  He is either **broke** or **busy**.

Try It

A. Complete each sentence with an adjective from the box.

empty	excited	sensible	shocked

1. Ivan is excited about buying new running shoes.
2. Juan is shocked by the prices at the store.
3. Juan is sensible about spending his money.
4. Ivan's bank account is sometimes empty.

B. Complete each sentence. Use predicate adjectives. Possible responses:

5. At the athletic store, the shoes are trendy but expensive.
6. At the discount store, the shoes are boring or cheap.
7. Juan will choose shoes that are practical.
8. Ivan spends his money on shoes that are fashionable and unique.

Write It

C. Answer the questions about spending habits. Use predicate adjectives.

9. How do you handle your money? I ______________________________.

10. Do you have a friend who likes to save his or her money? Describe him or her. This friend ______________________________.

11. Describe a friend who spends more than he or she saves. My friend ______________________________ ______________________________.

12. Describe a purchase you made recently. I bought ______________________________. It is ______________________________.

D. (13–16) Write at least four sentences about spending or saving money. Use predicate adjectives.

____

____

____

____

____

Edit It

E. (17–20) Edit the journal entry. Fix the four missing predicate adjectives. Possible responses:

August 17

Today, I went shopping with Ivan. He is careless with his money. He spent a lot on shoes that are ^cool. The prices at his store are ^high. Then we went to the discount store. The shoes there are ^cheap but nice. I guess he likes to spend his money. I like to save it. I am ^careful with my money!

Proofreader's Marks

Add text:

This is ^expensive.

See all Proofreader's Marks on page ix.

Name ________________________________ Date ______________

64 Why Do You Use a Demonstrative Adjective?

To Point Something Out

- A **demonstrative adjective** signals where something is—either near or far.
- Use **this** and **these** for something near to you.

  My Aunt Sharon is buying **this fabric** here.

  These buttons are beautiful.
- Use **that** and **those** for something far from you.

  I will buy **that pattern** over there for sewing.

  She will show me how to make **those shirts** over there in the display.

	Demonstrative Adjectives	
	Singular	**Plural**
Near	this	these
Far	that	those

Try It

A. Complete each sentence about a new interest. Use demonstrative adjectives.

1. I like to design clothes. I like ____this____ fabric here.

2. There are patterns for skirts and dresses on ____that____ shelf on the other side of the store.

3. The clerk points to ____that____ fabric on the wall.

4. I look closely at ____these____ shirts here to study the way the sleeves have been designed.

5. I also want to look at ____that____ dress in the shop across the street.

6. Aunt Sharon asks what material is used in ____this____ dress here.

7. I will base my design on ____those____ patterns over there.

B. **Complete each sentence about an interest that could become a career. Write the correct demonstrative adjective.**

8. I had so much fun. I realized that ______this______ (this / these) career is the one for me.

9. ______Those______ (These / Those) patterns over there are my own unique designs.

10. My Aunt Sharon told me to go to ______that______ (this / that) store across town.

11. I can make anything with ______this______ (this / these) sewing machine in my room.

12. I will look into ______that______ (this / that) design school on the other side of town.

13. ______These______ (These / Those) courses here in the school catalog look interesting.

Write It

C. **You have a friend with an interest that he or she can develop into a career. Answer the questions about your friend. Use demonstrative adjectives.**

14. What is your friend's interest? My friend's interest ____________________

____________________.

15. What school courses will help him or her get more skills? My friend will need to study

____________________.

16. Does this career interest you? Why or why not? ____________________

____

D. (17–20) **Write at least four sentences to tell about an interest that you could turn into a career.**

____

____

____

____

____

Name ______________________ Date ____________

65 Use Adjectives to Elaborate

Remember: Use adjectives to add interesting, lively details to your writing. Adjectives help readers see, hear, touch, smell, and taste.

See	Hear	Touch	Smell	Taste
colorful	loud	crunchy	clean	salty
ripe	metallic	smooth	earthy	sour
shiny	tapping	soft	fresh	sweet

The ^purple plums in the ^shiny bowl will add a ^tangy flavor to this ^delicious recipe.

Try It

A. Complete each sentence. Add adjectives to elaborate. Possible responses:

1. Ms. Bruno picks ___fresh___ vegetables from her garden.
2. She uses the tomatoes to make ___spicy___ spaghetti sauce.
3. Ms. Bruno chops the ingredients with a ___sharp___ knife.
4. A ___chewy___ bread will complete the meal.

B. Complete each sentence. Add an adjective from the category in parentheses. Use adjectives from the chart or your own. Possible responses:

5. Ms. Bruno served me ___spicy___ food that made my tongue feel hot. **(taste)**
6. She thinks take-out food is too ___salty___. **(taste)**
7. This crunchy peanut butter gives the sandwiches a ___rough___ texture. **(touch)**
8. Ms. Bruno's fruit salad includes ___bright___ colors. **(see)**
9. Cut lemons give the kitchen a ___fresh___ smell. **(smell)**

Write It

C. Answer these questions about food. Use adjectives in your answers.

10. What is your favorite homemade food? I like ____________________ because it tastes ____.

11. What is your favorite take-out food? ____

12. How does your favorite dessert taste? ____

13. What is your favorite snack food? Why do you like it? ____________________
____

D. (14–16) **Write at least three sentences about whether you prefer homemade food or take-out food and why. Use adjectives in your sentences.**

____
____
____
____

Edit It

E. (17–20) **Improve the journal entry. Add four adjectives to elaborate.** Possible responses:

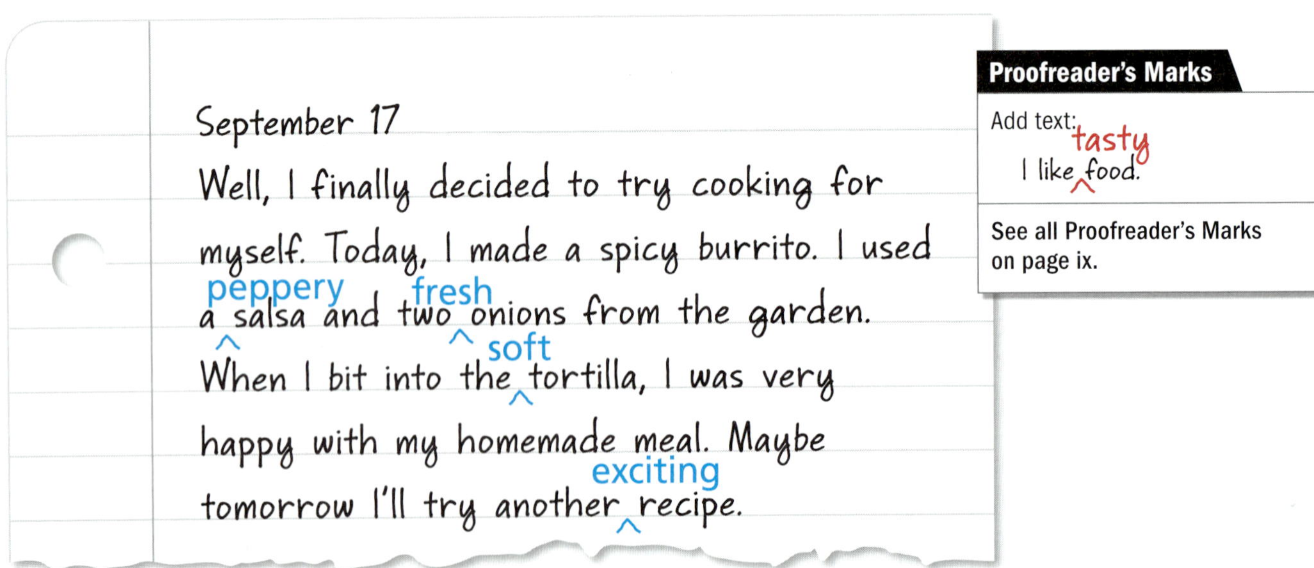

Name ______________________ Date ____________

66 Can You Use an Adjective to Make a Comparison?

Yes, But You Have to Change the Adjective.

- Use a **comparative adjective** to compare two people, places, or things.

  Jared's present is **large**, but my present is **larger**.

  The necklace is **more beautiful** than the bracelet.

- There are two ways to turn an adjective into a comparative adjective:

1. If the adjective has one syllable, add **-er**. If it has two syllables and ends in a consonant + **y**, change the **y** to i before you add **-er**.	**smart** **smarter**	**small** **smaller**	**pretty** **prettier**
2. Use **more** before most other two-syllable adjectives. If the adjective has three or more syllables, use **more**.	**anxious** **more anxious**		**responsible** **more responsible**

Try It

A. Complete each sentence with a comparative adjective.

1. That present will make Inga happy, but this one will make her happier.
2. This gift is cool, but the other gift is cooler.
3. I am excited about her birthday, but Inga is more excited about it.
4. I had a hard time making my decision, and you had a harder time.
5. We were nervous about choosing a gift, but Jared was even more nervous.

B. **Write the comparative form of the adjective in parentheses.**

6. The necklace is more expensive than the earrings. **(expensive)**

7. The chain on the gold necklace is thicker than the chain on the silver necklace. **(thick)**

8. This charm is smaller than that charm. **(small)**

9. Your present is more special than what you gave her last year. **(special)**

10. Inga is more gracious about receiving gifts than I am. **(gracious)**

11. Which of these two necklaces looks prettier? **(pretty)**

12. The note you wrote in the card is longer than the note I wrote. **(long)**

Write It

C. **Answer the questions to tell about a time when you bought a gift for a special friend or family member. Use comparative adjectives.**

13. What gift did you buy? I bought a ______________________.

14. What made your gift special? ______________________

____

15. What makes your friend or family member special? ______________________

____

16. Was the person happy with your gift? Explain. ______________________

____

D. (17–20) **Write at least four sentences to compare two items that you might like to buy for someone special. What makes you choose one item over the other? Use comparative adjectives.**

____

____

____

____

____

Name ______________________ Date ____________

67 Can an Adjective Compare More Than Two Things?

Yes, But You Have to Use a Different Form.

- A **superlative adjective** compares three or more people, places, or things. To turn an adjective into a superlative adjective:

1. Add **-est** to a one-syllable adjective or to a two-syllable adjective that ends in a consonant + **y**.	It was **the roughest** trail I ever tried to ride. This is **the rockiest** trail in the county.
2. Use **most** before most other two-syllable adjectives. Use **most** before an adjective of three or more syllables.	Only **the most steadfast** bikers try it. It was **the most challenging** trail I ever tried to ride.

- Use **the** before the superlative.
- Never use **more** and **-er** together. Never use **most** and **-est** together.

It was the ~~most~~ roughest trail I ever tried.

Try It

A. **Complete each sentence with the correct superlative adjective.**

1. I went mountain biking on the steepest trail in the state park.
steep / steepest

2. The first part of the trail was the most treacherous of all.
more treacherous / most treacherous

3. I was not the slowest person in our group.
slower / slowest

4. My friend Sam was the fastest of all on the straightaways.
faster/ fastest

5. Climbing up the hills was the hardest part of the trail ride.
harder/ hardest

B. **Complete each sentence. Use the correct superlative form of an adjective from the box.**

challenging	cool	dirty	easy	experienced	rocky	thrilling

6. The group leader was the most experienced rider of all the participants.

7. The easiest way down the mountain was on the paved road.

8. The turns were the most challenging part of the course.

9. I thought the steep slopes were the most thrilling of all.

10. After riding through the puddles, our bikes were the dirtiest in the group.

11. I just missed the rockiest part of all when I went off the trail.

12. I think this trail is the coolest trail I have been on.

Write It

C. **Answer the questions about an intense athletic activity. Use superlative adjectives.**

13. What is the most intense athletic activity? I think ________________ is the ________________________________.

14. What are the greatest physical challenges of this activity? ________________________________

15. What makes this a popular sport or activity? ________________________________

D. **(16–20) Write at least five sentences comparing two intense athletic activities. Use superlative adjectives.**

____

____

____

____

____

Name ______________________ Date ____________

68 Which Adjectives Are Irregular?

Good, Bad, Many, Much, and Little

- Some adjectives have special forms.

To Describe 1 Thing	good	bad	many / much	few	little
To Compare 2 Things	better	worse	more	fewer	less
To Compare 3 or More Things	best	worst	most	fewest	least

- Use **many** or **few** to describe things you can count. Use **much** or **little** to describe things you can't count. Some words can be either count or noncount, depending on usage.

  How **many** confrontations have you had on the court?

  How **much** confrontation in a game is too much?

Try It

A. Complete each sentence. Write the correct irregular comparative adjective.

1. I told Kyra she is the ___most___ (more / most) talented player on the team.
2. Kyra felt like the ___worst___ (worse / worst) player of all.
3. Kyra has ___more___ (more / most) defensive skills than Michelle.
4. She is ___better___ (good / better) than Luanne at free throws.

B. Write the correct form of good, bad, many, much, few, or little. Possible responses:

5. Kyra feels ___bad___ about the first set of tryouts.
6. I told her the second tryout would be ___better___ than the first.
7. She made ___fewer___ mistakes than Michelle.
8. She has the ___best___ offensive skills of all of the athletes.

Write It

C. You have a friend who is worried about trying out for a team. Answer the questions. Use irregular comparative adjectives.

9. What do you say to encourage your friend? I tell him/her that _______________.

10. How could your friend improve his/her skills? _______________

11. What do you tell your friend if he or she doesn't make the team? _______________

____

12. Why is it good to keep trying? _______________

____

D. (13–16) Write at least four sentences comparing the skills and talents of three people on a school team. Use irregular comparative adjectives.

____

____

____

____

____

Edit It

E. (17–20) Edit the letter. Fix four irregular comparative adjectives.

Dear Kyra,

You are so good at basketball. You really are the best player on the team. You should feel strong, but you seem nervous. I think you have ~~least~~ less confidence than Sarah. You are the most talented player of all. I hope you feel ~~good~~ better about making the team than you did yesterday.

Good luck,

Emily

Proofreader's Marks

Add text:

She is the worst player on the team.

Change text:

You are ~~gooder~~ better than you think.

See all Proofreader's Marks on page ix.

Name ______________________ Date ______________

69 When Do You Use an Indefinite Adjective?

When You Can't Be Specific

- If you are not sure of the exact number or amount of something, use an **indefinite adjective**.

  I haven't spent **much** time with that group. **Some** people in that group are nice. **Many** people in that group do **a lot of** activities that my parents don't like.

- How do you know which adjective to use?

These adjectives go before a noun you can count, like **friends**:		These adjectives go before a noun you can't count, like **courage**:	
many	**a lot of**	**much**	**a lot of**
a few	**several**	**a little**	**not much**
some	**no**	**some**	**no**

Try It

A. Complete each sentence. Use indefinite adjectives from the chart. Possible responses:

1. I need a lot of, much courage when I talk to my parents about my friends.
2. They like most of my friends, but they think a few, some kids are not good for me.
3. They don't want me to spend a lot of, much time with these friends.

B. Write the correct indefinite adjective to complete each sentence.

4. Several (**Several / A little**) friends do positive and healthy activities.
5. A few (**A few / Much**) friends are not good role models.
6. Several (**Several / Much**) friends are reckless sometimes.
7. I know there are many (**many / much**) reasons to tell my parents the truth about them.

Write It

C. **Answer the questions about a time when you needed to tell your parents the truth. Use indefinite adjectives.**

8. What did you need to tell your parents? I told them that I ____________________.

9. What was difficult about talking to your parents? ____________________

10. What was a benefit of telling your parents the truth? ____________________

____

11. Why is it difficult to tell the truth sometimes? ____________________

____

D. **(12–15) Write at least four sentences about the benefits and difficulties of telling the truth to your parents. Use indefinite adjectives.**

____

____

____

____

____

Edit It

E. **(16–20) Edit the letter. Fix five indefinite adjectives.** Possible responses:

Dear Mom and Dad,

Thanks for spending some time talking about my friendships with me. At first, I agreed with only ~~no~~ a few points that you made. Now, I understand you want me to have ~~much~~ many good friendships. I should not spend ~~several~~ much time with people who are not making healthy decisions. We have had ~~a little~~ several good conversations this past year. I have ~~many~~ a lot of / much appreciation for your advice.

Love,

Denise

Proofreader's Marks

Change text:

I have ~~much~~ several good friends.

See all Proofreader's Marks on page ix.

Name ______________________ Date ____________

70 Use Adjectives Correctly

Remember: You can use adjectives to describe or compare people, places, or things.

- How do you know which adjective to use?

To Describe 1 Thing	loud	difficult	good	many/ much
To Compare 2 Things	louder	more difficult	better	more
To Compare 3 or More Things	loudest	most difficult	best	most

Try It

A. Complete each sentence with the correct adjective.

1. The recent hurricane was the ___most damaging___ (**more damaging/most damaging**) storm in the town's history.

2. After the storm, people had ___some___ (**a few/some**) doubt that the neighborhood would ever be livable again.

3. ___Many___ (**Many/Much**) students wanted to help the people whose homes were damaged.

4. Will the new houses make this a ___better___ (**best/better**) neighborhood than it was before?

B. (5–8) Complete the paragraph by writing adjectives in the correct form. Possible responses:

The old houses needed improvements. It was ___a lot of___ work. Everyone helped out. We made ___many___ decisions together during the project. Some people were ___better___ than others at different tasks. I liked the sense of teamwork. It was the ___most rewarding___ experience of my whole life.

Write It

C. **Your friends and you volunteer to help build a house for a family in need. Answer these questions. Use adjectives correctly to describe or compare.**

9. What is the most important reason for helping others? I think that ______________________

______________________.

10. How does your work help make life better for the family in need? ______________________

____

11. What do you learn from the experience? ______________________

D. **(12–15) Write at least four sentences describing a service project teens can participate in at home or school. Use adjectives correctly.**

____

____

____

____

Edit It

E. **(16–20) Edit the journal entry. Fix the five mistakes with adjectives.** Possible responses:

July 20

I had a lot of enthusiasm about this service project. One family's house was in the ~~bad~~ worst condition of all. The work was ~~most hard~~ harder than the work I did last summer. There was only ~~a few~~ a little time to rest—only ~~a little~~ a few minutes each day. But watching the family move into their new house was the ~~satisfyingest~~ most satisfying part of the whole experience for me.

Proofreader's Marks

Change text:

We like doing ~~many~~ a lot of work.

See all Proofreader's Marks on page ix.

Name ______________________ Date ____________

71 Why Do You Need Adverbs?

To Tell *How*, *When*, or *Where*

- Use an **adverb** to describe a verb. Adverbs often end in **-ly**.
  In driving school, I learned to drive **carefully** in uncertain conditions. (how)
  I learned to apply the brakes **immediately** if a light turned yellow. (when)
  I also learned to pull **up** the parking brake. (where)

- Use an **adverb** to make an adjective or another adverb stronger.
  I drive **very** carefully.
  another adverb
  I was **extremely** nervous driving in the rain.
  adjective

- Adverbs add details and bring life to your writing.
  When the car skidded, I reacted **calmly**.
  I'm glad I listened **closely** to my driving instructor.

Try It

A. Complete each sentence. Use adverbs to add details. Possible responses:

1. The other cars swerved dangerously on the road.
2. I held firmly onto the steering wheel.
3. The car in front of me moved quickly out of the way.
4. I pressed my foot down on the brakes.
5. I drove safely away from the cars in front of us.
6. I stopped briefly to calm down.
7. I understood instantly that I had avoided an accident.

B. **Add details to the story. Choose from the adverbs in the box.**

exactly	extremely	lightly	patiently	very

8. One car slowed down and nearly stopped before it lightly hit another car's bumper.

9. I was extremely frightened as the events unfolded.

10. I acted very quickly in that situation.

11. I was happy that I knew exactly what to do.

12. A woman asked patiently if I was okay.

Write It

C. **Your friend reacts well during a moment of crisis while driving. Imagine you are with him or her. Answer the questions. Use adverbs to add details.**

13. What is the best way to react during a moment of crisis? I think ______________________________
______________________________.

14. What can you do to help your friend in this situation? I can help by ______________________________
______________________________.

15. What is an unhelpful way to react during a crisis? ______________________________

16. What do you learn about yourself or your friend after this uncertain situation? ______________
____

D. **(17–20) Write at least four sentences to describe a situation in which you reacted well in a moment of crisis or an uncertain situation. What did you learn about yourself?**

____
____
____
____
____

Name ______________________ Date ______________

72 What Happens When You Add *Not* to a Sentence?

You Make the Sentence Negative.

- The word not is an adverb. Add it to a sentence to make it negative.
  If the verb is an **action verb**, change the sentence like this:
  My mom **wants** me to help Mr. Bobera.
  My mom **does** not **want** me to watch television.
- If the verb is a form of **be**, just place not after the verb:
  Mr. Bobera **is** our elderly neighbor. He **is** not very active.
- When you shorten a verb plus not, replace the **o** in not with an apostrophe.

1. Mom **does not** want Mr. Bobera to do heavy lifting.
   Mom **doesn't** want Mr. Bobera to do heavy lifting.
2. I **can not** let him do the work alone.
   I **can't** let him do the work alone.

Try It

A. Rewrite each sentence to make it negative. Use the adverb not.

1. Mr. Bobera is lazy. Mr. Bobera is not (isn't) lazy.
2. He asks for help. He does not (doesn't) ask for help.
3. At first, I like helping him with his yard and house.
   At first, I do not (don't) like helping him with his yard and house.

B. Complete each sentence. Use the adverb not.

4. Mr. Bobera is not (isn't) boring.
5. He can not (can't) do many things, but he knows a lot.
6. He does not (doesn't) have a strong voice, but he tells interesting stories.
7. I did not (didn't) earn money helping him, but I gained a good friend and mentor.

Write It

C. **Think about things you like and dislike (activities, sports, chores, foods). Answer the questions. Use the adverb not in some of your sentences.**

8. Name one thing you like and another thing you do not like. I like ______________, but I ______________________________.

9. Is there something you do not like but that you know is good for you? Explain.

____

10. What have you gained from doing something you initially did not like? ______________

____

D. **(11–15) Write at least five sentences comparing one thing you like with one thing you do not like. Use the adverb not in some of your sentences.**

____

____

____

____

____

Edit It

E. **(16–20) Edit the journal entry. Fix five of the adverbs.**

April 4

I didn't know why Mom asked me to help Mr. Bobera on a Saturday. I [don't] think working on Saturdays is fun. At first, I ~~didnot~~ [didn't] want to go. Then, I saw he ~~can~~ [can't] do much on his own. He wanted to pay me, but I did [not] want it. He is now my good friend. He is [not] just a neighbor.

Proofreader's Marks

Add text:

He is [not] a boring person.

Change text:

Mr. Bobera ~~can~~ [can't] lift heavy things.

See all Proofreader's Marks on page ix.

Name ______________________ Date ______________

73 How Do You Make a Sentence Negative?

Use One, and Only One, Negative Word.

- These words are negative words: **no**, **nobody**, **nothing**, **no one**, **not**, **never**, **nowhere**, and **none**.
- Use only one negative word in a sentence.

Incorrect:	No one went nowhere before the test.
Correct:	No one went anywhere before the test.
Incorrect:	After the bell rang, nobody could do nothing more.
Correct:	After the bell rang, nobody could do anything more.
Incorrect:	I didn't have no idea that the test would be so long.
Correct:	I didn't have any idea that the test would be so long.
Correct:	I had no idea that the test would be so long.

Try It

A. (1–6) Edit the journal entry. Use only one negative word in each sentence.

November 15

I studied all weekend. I never worked on anything so much. I didn't want ~~no~~ any help preparing for the test. I ~~wasn't~~ was focused on my task like nothing else I had ever done. Nobody could make me think about ~~nothing~~ anything else. I walked into the classroom. I didn't want to be ~~nowhere~~ anywhere else. Nothing could ~~not~~ stop me from writing until the bell rang. When I got the results, I couldn't ~~never~~ believe it. I got the highest score!

Proofreader's Marks

Change text:

We didn't have to do ~~nothing~~ anything but study.

Delete:

I can't ~~never~~ believe it.

See all Proofreader's Marks on page ix.

B. **Rewrite each sentence. Use only one negative word.** Possible responses:

7. I was never not so happy about a test.
I was never so happy about a test.

8. Nobody did no better than I did.
Nobody did better than I did.

9. I didn't have no idea that I would do so well.
I didn't have any idea that I would do so well.

10. On the weekend after the test, I didn't want to do nothing.
On the weekend after the test, I didn't want to do anything.

11. I would not have no more worries.
I would not have any more worries.

12. Never again will I worry about no test that much.
Never again will I worry about any test that much.

Write It

C. **Have you ever expected to perform poorly and then learned later that you succeeded? Answer the questions. Use only one negative word in each sentence.**

13. What made you think you would not perform well? ______________________

14. What can you do to prepare for a stressful situation or test? ______________

15. What could you do to help a friend who is worried about a test or competition? ________

____

D. **(16–20) Write at least five sentences about something negative that you turned into a positive experience. Use only one negative word in each sentence.**

____

____

____

____

____

Name ______________________ Date ______________

74 Can You Use an Adverb to Make a Comparison?

Yes, But You Need to Change the Adverb.

- Adverbs have different forms. Use the form that fits your purpose.

To Describe 1 Action	hard	quickly	well	badly
To Compare 2 Actions	harder	more quickly	better	worse
To Compare 3 or More Actions	hardest	most quickly	best	worst

- How many things are being compared in these sentences?

  I wrote **worse** than my friend did.

  I decided to work **the hardest** of all my friends to excel at writing.

Try It

A. Write the correct adverb to describe the action in each sentence.

1. I checked my drafts __more carefully__ than I had the first time.
more carefully / most carefully

2. I worked __harder__ than my friends did.
harder / more hard

3. One teacher helped me the __most patiently__ of all.
more patiently / most patiently

4. Mr. Hingis advised me to plan my writing __better__ than I had been doing.
better / best

5. I really wanted to write __more creatively__ than I did last year.
creatively / more creatively

B. Write the correct form of the adverb in parentheses to complete each sentence.

6. I did __worse__ at grammar than at story ideas. **(badly)**

7. I learned that I did __best__ of all at being imaginative. **(well)**

8. Now, I work __more carefully__ than I did before. **(carefully)**

9. I am writing __more clearly__ after taking Mr. Hingis's class. **(clearly)**

Write It

C. Answer the questions about a friend of yours. Use adverbs that compare.

10. What do you do better than your friend? I ________________________________.

11. What skill or talent does your friend do better than you? My friend is ________________________________.

12. What does it take to be the best at doing something? ________________________________

13. Describe a time when you discovered that hard work pays off. ________________________________

D. (14–16) **Write at least three sentences to tell about something you would like to improve about yourself in the next year. Use adverbs that compare.**

____

____

____

____

Edit It

E. (17–20) **Edit the journal entry. Fix four adverbs that compare.**

September 22

My Goals for the New School Year

English: I work well on short assignments. I need to do [better] this year than last year on long essays.

Math: I should work [more] carefully on my homework than I did last year.

Science: I work ~~faster~~ [fastest] of all in the labs. I clean up the ~~better~~ [worst] of all. I need to improve this.

Proofreader's Marks

Add text:
You helped me [most] of all.

Change text:
I work ~~most~~ [more] patiently than I did last year.

See all Proofreader's Marks on page ix.

Name ______________________ Date ____________

75 Use Adverbs Correctly

Remember: You can use adverbs to describe and compare actions. An adverb can also make another adverb or adjective stronger.

Describe	Compare	Make Stronger
I sat **quietly** waiting for the results.	I reacted **more calmly** than my friend did.	The school election results are **completely** surprising to me.
The students cheered **enthusiastically**.	I think **best** when I am relaxed.	The assembly hall is **very** noisy.

Try It

A. Write adverbs to add details to the sentences. Possible responses:

1. I stood up ___slowly___ when the principal said my name.
2. I reacted ___more quietly___ than the other candidates.
3. The cheers for me were ___extremely___ loud.
4. I ___suddenly___ realized that I was voted class president.
5. I was ___very___ grateful to all of the people who voted for me.
6. Afterward, a student said I spoke the ___best___ of all the candidates.

B. Write the correct adverb to complete each sentence.

7. My election team worked ___harder___ than the other team.
   hard / harder
8. I focused ___more___ intently on the issues than the other candidate.
   more / most
9. The support I got from my classmates made me ___incredibly___ proud.
   incredible / incredibly
10. I realized that I succeed ___best___ of all when I really believe in something.
    better / best

Write It

C. Answer these questions about the importance of personal accomplishments. Use adverbs correctly to describe or compare actions.

11. Compare two students you know who compete with each other in a sport or school activity. ______________________

____

12. How can being good at something make a big change in your life? ______________________

____

13. When have you felt that something you accomplished was going to change your life for the better? ______________________

____

D. (14–17) Write at least four sentences describing your friends and comparing their talents, skills, or personalities. Use adverbs in your sentences.

____

____

____

____

____

Edit It

E. (18–20) Edit the newsletter. Fix the three mistakes with adverbs. Possible responses:

Haven School Newsletter

The students voted individually in the voting booths last Friday. They ~~careful~~ carefully considered all of the candidates. Out of all of the choices, Annie Broderick ~~more~~ most impressed the student body. The teachers are ~~extreme~~ extremely proud of her and the other candidates for their hard work. Congratulations, Annie!

Proofreader's Marks

Change text:

She campaigned ~~better~~ best of all.

See all Proofreader's Marks on page ix.

Name ______________________ Date ____________

Edit and Proofread

Capitalize Quotations Correctly

When quoting only part of a sentence, capitalize the first word of the quotation only if it is:

- a proper noun, such as Amy Tan or China

  As a Chinese American writer, "**Amy Tan** often explores immigration themes," such as the conflict between a Chinese-born mother and her American-born daughter.

- the first word of a sentence and you are quoting the entire sentence

  Thus, the mother says to Jing-mei in Chinese: "**Only** one kind of daughter can live in this house. Obedient daughter!"

This rule also applies to poetry. Whether or not you capitalize the first word, the rest of the quotation should follow the poet's capitalization.

The speaker urges readers to guard their "dreams / **For** when dreams go / **Life** is a barren field / **Frozen** with snow."

The word **dreams** is not capitalized because it is not a proper noun or the first word of the sentence.

The speaker urges readers, "**Hold** fast to dreams / **For** when dreams go / **Life** is a barren field / **Frozen** with snow."

The word **Hold** is capitalized because it is the first word of the sentence and all of the sentence is being quoted.

Try It

Proofreader's Marks

Capitalize:

The poem says, "life is a barren field."

Do not capitalize:

Tan says that relationships form "The heart of her work."

A. Use proofreader's marks to correct the capitalization errors.

1. Robert Frost is "One of the most widely read and celebrated poets in American history."
2. He believed a poem "Begins in delight and ends in wisdom."
3. In his poem "The Road Not Taken," the speaker must make a choice, "Two roads diverged in a yellow wood / and sorry I could not travel both."
4. In the end, the speaker admits, "Oh, I kept the first for another day! / yet knowing how way leads on to way / I doubted if I should ever come back."

Name ______________________ Date ______________

Use Quotation Marks Correctly

- Put quotation marks around the exact phrase or sentence that you quote from a source.

  Naomi Shihab Nye's poems "**combine** transcendent liveliness and sparkle along with warmth and human insight."

- Do not use quotation marks if you are paraphrasing, or describing what a person said.

  Her poems combine a lively energy with warmth and personal insight.

Try It

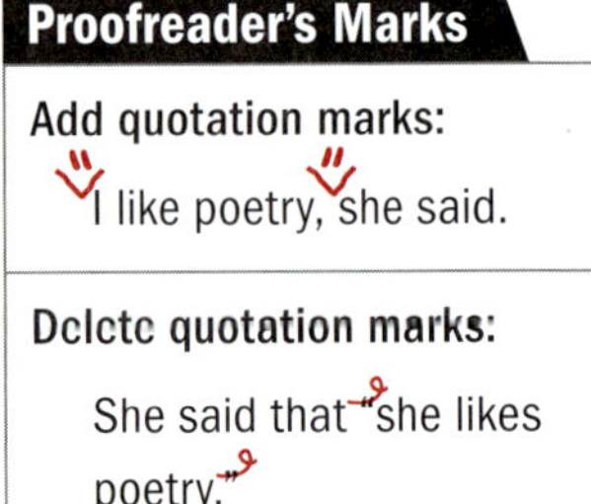

A. Edit each sentence. Add or delete quotation marks as necessary.

5. Naomi Shihab Nye is a "poet, essayist, and novelist."

6. The *School Library Journal* said, The author has the ability to perceive and describe her surroundings so skillfully that readers are drawn into these experiences and are enriched in the process.

7. The critic said, Nye gives voice to her experience as an Arab-American through poems about heritage and peace that overflow with a humanitarian spirit.

8. In her poem "Remembered," the speaker says, As if objects could listen / As if earth had a memory, too.

9. The poem describes "how an old man hopes to be remembered."

B. (10–15) **Write at least six sentences about your favorite poem or story. Describe the style of writing and what you like about the piece. Include information about the author. Be sure to use quotation marks correctly.**

____

____

____

____

____

Name ______________________ Date ____________

✓ Check for Parallel Structure

Combining shorter sentences into one longer sentence adds variety to your writing. When combining sentences, be sure that similar elements in your sentences are parallel in form. For instance, if you have two or more ideas in the predicate, make sure they have the same word pattern.

Incorrect: Langston Hughes was a poet, a playwright, and liked jazz music.

Correct: Langston Hughes was **a poet**, **a playwright**, and **a jazz enthusiast**.

Try It

A. **Rewrite each sentence so that it has parallel structure.**

16. Langston Hughes wrote poetry, created plays, and was enjoying jazz music. Langston Hughes wrote poetry, created plays, and enjoyed jazz music.

17. He was born in Missouri, growing up in Illinois, and eventually settling in Ohio. He was born in Missouri, grew up in Illinois, and eventually settled in Ohio.

18. Hughes attended high school in Cleveland, Ohio, where he edited the yearbook, was writing for the school newspaper, and began to author stories and plays. Hughes attended high school in Cleveland, Ohio, where he edited the yearbook, wrote for the school newspaper, and began to author stories and plays.

19. In Hughes's earlier poems, he presents dreams that are hopeful and alive, but in his later work, he is writing about a dream that is neglected. In Hughes's earlier poems, he presents dreams that are hopeful and alive, but in his later work, he writes about a dream that is neglected.

20. Hughes evokes dreams so real that people can hold them, nurturing them, and follow them to freedom. Hughes evokes dreams so real that people can hold them, nurture them, and follow them to freedom.

Name ______________________ Date ______________

Edit and Proofread

✓ Use Adjectives and Adverbs Correctly

- Use a **comparative adjective** to show how two things are alike or different. Add **-er** to one-syllable adjectives or to two-syllable adjectives that end in a consonant + **y**. Then add **than**. Use **more** or **less** with most other two-syllable adjectives and with adjectives of three syllables or more.

  Incorrect: Alejandra's research report is more long than Daniel's.

  Correct: Alejandra's research report is **longer than** Daniel's.

  Incorrect: Lee's reflective essay is interestinger than Renee's.

  Correct: Lee's reflective essay is **more interesting than** Renee's.

- Use an **adverb** to describe a verb or make an adjective or another adverb stronger. Do not use an adjective instead of an adverb. Remember that adverbs often end in **-ly**.

  Incorrect: Claire wrote her research report quick.

  Correct: Claire wrote her research report **quickly**.

Try It

A. **Choose the correct form of the adjective or adverb in each sentence.**

21. Langston Hughes was an ___amazingly___ gifted poet and writer.
amazing / amazingly

22. To me, his poems are ___more inspiring___ than those of any other poet of his generation.
inspiringer / more inspiring

23. The treatment of dreams in Hughes's earlier poetry contrasts ___sharply___ with the treatment of dreams in his later poetry.
sharp / sharply

24. His poem "The Dream Keeper" is ___happier___ than some of his later poems about dreams.
happier / more happy

25. In one of his later poems, "A Dream Deferred," he presents dreams in a ___harsher___ light than he did in earlier poems.
harsher / more harsh

Name ______________________ Date ____________

76 What's a Simple Sentence?

A Sentence with One Subject and One Predicate

You can express a complete thought with a simple sentence.
In statements, the subject usually comes before the predicate.

Subject	Predicate
Teenagers (noun)	**are** (verb) our future leaders.
Teachers (noun)	**mentor** (verb) teens and **prepare** (verb) them for college.
Mothers (noun) and **fathers** (noun)	**guide** (verb) teens.
They (pronoun)	**prepare** (verb) them for adulthood.

Try It

A. Complete each sentence by adding a subject or a predicate. Possible responses:

1. my sister and I My sister and I are teenagers.
2. are an important part of society We are an important part of society.
3. want a lot of responsibility Most teenagers want a lot of responsibility.
4. responsibility Responsibility teaches life lessons.
5. grow up to be responsible adults Responsible teens grow up to be responsible adults.
6. every adult in the world Every adult in the world was a teenager once.

B. **Form complete sentences. Combine each group of words with a subject or predicate. Circle the complete subject and underline the complete predicate.** Possible responses:

7. went to a leadership program in Washington, D.C. (I) went to a leadership program in Washington, D.C.

8. teens from all around the world. (Teens from all around the world) were there with me.

9. our civic responsibilities. (Our civic responsibilities) were an important part of the program.

10. my favorite activity. (My favorite activity) was our visit to Congress.

11. toured the House of Representatives and the Senate. (Our group) toured the House of Representatives and the Senate.

12. the teens in this program. (The teens in this program) might be future senators or representatives one day.

Write It

C. **Use complete sentences to answer the questions.**

13. What is one of your responsibilities? ______

14. How does it prepare you for adulthood? ______

15. What adult is a role model for you? ______

16. How does that adult prepare you for adult responsibilities? ______

D. **(17–20) Write at least four complete sentences that tell more about responsibilities that prepare teens for adulthood.**

Name ______________________ Date ____________

77 What's an Infinitive?

To + a Verb

Use **to** plus a **verb** to form an **infinitive**. An infinitive acts like a noun, an adjective, or an adverb.

- **Like all nouns, an infinitive can be the object of an action verb.**

  Mom **decides** (verb) **to go** (infinitive) shopping. What teen **wants** (verb) **to go** (infinitive) shopping?

- You can also use an infinitive in the **subject** of a sentence. The **verb** will always be singular.

  To go (infinitive) grocery shopping **is** (verb) not fun. **To go** (infinitive) **clothes shopping** **interests** (verb) **me.**

- You can also use an infinitive as an adjective or an adverb.

  I often **have** (verb) a desire **to shop** (infinitive as an adjective). I **shop** (verb) **to buy** (infinitive as an adverb) clothes.

Try It

A. Complete each sentence with an infinitive. Possible responses:

1. Many teens want ___to be___ more independent.
2. ___To be___ more independent usually means taking on more responsibility.
3. Some teens want ___to work___ part-time.
4. They try ___to earn___ as much money as they can.

B. (5–11) Complete each sentence with an infinitive. Possible responses:

___To be___ a teen is not all that bad. For example, teens are able ___to drive___, but ___to pay___ the car insurance is rarely their responsibility. They have the right ___to hold___ a job but don't pay a lot of taxes. They eat dinner every night, but ___to cook___ it is usually someone else's chore. They have a home ___to live___ in, but ___to pay___ the rent is not their worry.

Write It

C. Complete each sentence about people in your life who have responsibilities that benefit you. Use an infinitive in each sentence.

12. It's my father's responsibility to ______________________________.

13. It's my mother's responsibility ______________________________.

14. It's my parents' responsibility ______________________________.

15. It's my teachers' responsibility ______________________________.

16. It's my coach's responsibility ______________________________.

D. (17–20) Write at least four sentences about responsibilities that adults have that teens do not have. Use an infinitive in each sentence.

____

____

____

____

____

Edit It

E. (21–25) Edit the journal entry. Fix the five mistakes with infinitives.

August 24

I plan to take my driver's test today. Finally, I will be able ^to drive! Once I can drive, I want ^to be more helpful. To ~~helps~~ ^help my mom in every way I can ~~are~~ ^is something I've always done. My mom will help me, too. She will pay for my auto insurance. To buy auto insurance ~~are~~ ^is expensive, and I'm glad that she will pay for that!

Proofreader's Marks

Add text:

I want ^to drive.

Change text:

To drive a car ~~are~~ ^is expensive.

See all Proofreader's Marks on page ix.

Name ______________________ Date ____________

78 Can a Verb Act Like a Noun?

Yes, When It Is a Gerund.

Add **-ing** to a **verb** to form a **gerund.** A gerund acts like a noun in a sentence.

- A gerund is often the **object** of an **action verb**.

  I **like** (verb) **shopping** (gerund) for clothes. I manage some **shopping** every weekend.
  verb gerund

- You can also use a gerund as the **object** of a **preposition**.

  The thing **about shopping** (gerund) **is that it is a privilege.**

- Like all nouns, a gerund is often the **subject** of a sentence. The **verb** will always be singular.

  Shopping (gerund) **is** (verb) not a right. **Earning** (gerund) money **allows** (verb) **me to shop.**

Try It

A. **Complete each sentence with a gerund using a verb from the box.** Possible responses:

have	rent	set	wish

1. Wishing for independence is what teens do best.

2. Jeff thinks renting his own apartment would be great for Michael.

3. Setting her own curfew is what Rosa longs for.

4. Having a shorter school day is Jenny's wish.

B. **(5–10) Complete each sentence with a gerund.**

Cole spends his days dreaming about getting his own car. His parents tell him to start working. Buying a car costs money. Wishing for a car won't help Cole to get one, but earning money will.

Write It

C. Teens have to be 18 to vote. Do you wish you could vote? Give your answer in four sentences. In each sentence, use the gerund form of the verb in parentheses.

11. (vote) ______________________________

12. (have) ______________________________

13. (turn) ______________________________

14. (cast my vote) ______________________________

D. (15–19) What rights and privileges do you wish you had? Write at least five sentences about your wishes. Use a gerund in each sentence.

____

____

____

____

____

____

Edit It

E. (20–25) Edit the letter. Fix the six mistakes in gerunds.

Dear Grandpa,

Being a teenager is so hard! ~~Have~~ Having to follow other people's rules all the time ~~are~~ is awful. Right now, I'm having a problem. I want to drive to the beach. Mom and Dad think that ~~drive~~ driving that far ~~are~~ is dangerous. I'm a good driver, though. I wish I could make my own decisions. ~~Talk~~ Talking to them ~~don't~~ doesn't help! Could you talk to them for me? Thanks.

Love,

Sandra

Proofreader's Marks

Change text:

~~Deal~~ Dealing with parents is hard!

See all Proofreader's Marks on page ix.

Name ______________________ Date ____________

79 What Do We Mean by Parallel Structure?

We Mean the Repetition of Patterns in a Sentence of Passage.

Parallel structure makes writing easier to understand.

Use parallel structure in your sentences: Put all the verbs in the same tense, and avoid mixing gerunds and infinitives.

To ignore a school bus's flashing lights is **to invite** tragedy.

Stopping at flashing lights and **waiting** are requirements.

Be sure to **stop**, **look** both ways, and **proceed** with caution.

To add power to your writing, use parallel structure in your longer passages.

I will show you that I can be responsible, that I can pass my driver's test, and that I can earn money to buy my own car.

Use parallel structure in lists.

- **Get** more babysitting and yard work jobs.
- **Put** 80% of the money I earn in the bank.
- **Search** online for used cars.

Try It

A. Complete each sentence using parallel structure. Possible responses:

1. I want to get more babysitting jobs, so I am going to ask Mrs. D'Allesandro to refer me to her friends.
2. She knows that I am good at caring for children, keeping them safe, and getting them to bed on time.

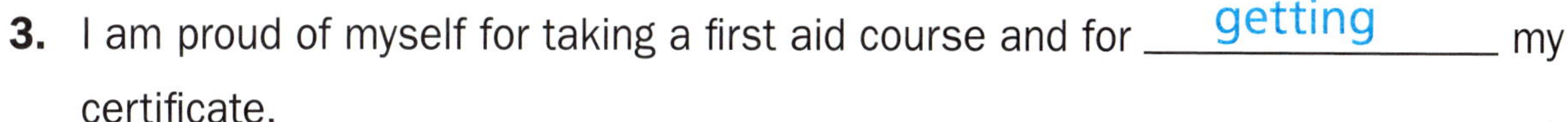

3. I am proud of myself for taking a first aid course and for getting my certificate.
4. Being responsible and having confidence in myself are helping me to find new jobs.

B. **Rewrite each sentence to reflect parallel structure.** Possible responses:

5. The D'Allesandro kids like watching TV, riding bikes, and to play board games.
The D'Allesandro kids like watching TV, riding bikes, and playing board games.

6. I plan to save most of my babysitting money, but I plan spending some of it on fun.
I plan to save most of my babysitting money, but I plan to spend some of it on fun.

7. To save most of my money and putting it in the bank will provide money for a car.
Saving most of my money and putting it in the bank will provide money for a car.

8. I want to buy a used car that runs well, will look okay, and doesn't cost too much.
I want to buy a used car that runs well, looks okay, and doesn't cost too much.

Write It

C. **Follow the directions. Use parallel structure in your answers.** Sentences will vary.

9. Name three skills you have that can help you get an after-school job. Use gerunds.
I am good at using a computer, making change, and being friendly.

10. Name three qualities you would like in a used car. Use infinitives.
I would like a car to look cool, to get good mileage, and to continue to work until I go to college.

D. **(11–15) Imagine that you want to buy a car of your own. List at least five steps you will take to do it. Be sure to use parallel structure in your list.**

Name ______________________ Date ____________

80 Vary Your Sentences

Remember: Your sentences are more interesting when you vary your word order and the types of sentences you write.

To vary your sentences, you can:

- Place a **verb** before the **subject**.

  There **are** many respectful **teens**. Rarely **do they cause** problems.

- Expand a sentence with an **infinitive phrase**.

  Many teens try. Many teens try **to behave respectfully**.

  Infinitive phrase

- Use an **infinitive** or a **gerund** as the subject of your sentence. Remember that these subjects always take a **singular verb**.

  To earn respect **requires** good behavior. **Working** hard **is** one way to earn respect.

  Infinitive / gerund

Try It

A. Rewrite each sentence. Change the word order, add an infinitive phrase, or use a gerund or an infinitive. Possible responses:

1. I drive carefully. I drive carefully to earn my parents' trust.
2. I complete my school work to make my parents respect me. Completing my school work makes my parents respect me.
3. I respect other people's rights so that they will respect mine. Respecting other people's rights makes them respect mine.
4. I can do many things to get people to respect me. There are many things I can do to get people to respect me.
5. Respect helps me. Respect helps me to get things I want.
6. Being respectful is an important quality. To be respectful is an important quality.

B. Edit each sentence. Fix gerunds, infinitives, verbs, or parallel structure. Possible responses:

7. Dressing nicely for work helps me ~~building~~ to build self-worth and to earn respect.

8. There ~~is~~ are times when I come in early or stay late.

9. I always work hard to impress my boss, too.

10. ~~Get~~ Getting my boss to like me and ~~to avoid~~ avoiding conflict are important.

11. One day I might need to get a recommendation.

12. To have a good recommendation ~~are~~ is important to me.

Proofreader's Marks

Change text:
There ~~is~~ are ways to earn respect.

Add text:
One way is to behave nicely.

See all Proofreader's Marks on page ix.

Write It

C. Complete each sentence. Tell what you do to earn respect. Use infinitives, gerunds, or a verb-subject word order.

13. Rarely ______________________________
______________________________.

14. To ______________________________
______________________________.

15. I try ______________________________
______________________________.

D. (16–20) Write at least five sentences about how teens can earn a community's trust and respect. Vary your word order. Use some gerunds and some infinitives.

____
____
____
____
____
____

Name ______________________ Date ____________

81 How Are Phrases and Clauses Different?

A Clause Has a Subject and a Predicate.

- A **phrase** is a group of words that function together. One sentence often has several phrases.

  Many **people** / at the restaurant / **believe** / strongly / in smoke-free air.

  noun phrase — adjective phrase — verb — adverb — adverb phrase

  This sentence is complete because it has a **subject** and a **verb**. A phrase never has both, so it does not express a complete thought.

- A **clause** contains a **subject** and a **verb**. An independent clause can stand alone as a sentence.

  Nonsmokers **want** to eat without breathing second-hand smoke.

- **Clauses** that begin with words like **when, because,** and **if** cannot stand alone.

  If **smokers** **want** to smoke and to eat at the same time

Try It

A. Decide which parts of each sentence are phrases. Write the phrases after the sentence. Separate them with commas.

1. Some people like to smoke their cigarettes in restaurants. Some people, to smoke their cigarettes, in restaurants

2. Other people want to eat without breathing cigarette smoke. Other people, to eat, without breathing cigarette smoke

3. Does one person's right to smoke cigarettes interfere with another person's right not to breathe the smoke? one person's right, to smoke cigarettes, with another person's right, not to breathe the smoke

4. Some states have passed laws to protect a nonsmoker's rights not to breathe second-hand smoke. Some states, to protect a nonsmoker's rights, not to breathe second-hand smoke

B. Rewrite each sentence. Include the phrase in parentheses in the right place in the new sentence.

5. Some people smoke cigarettes. **(at work)** Some people smoke cigarettes at work.

6. Many companies want this problem. **(to figure out a solution)** Many companies want to figure out a solution to this problem.

7. Some companies have separate areas to eat lunch. **(for smokers and nonsmokers)** Some companies have separate areas for smokers and nonsmokers to eat lunch.

8. Other companies have strict policies. **(about smoking in the building)** Other companies have strict policies about smoking in the building.

9. Smokers must go outside. **(to smoke their cigarettes)** Smokers must go outside to smoke their cigarettes.

Write It

C. What is your opinion on the right to smoke and the misuse of that right? Answer the questions. Use at least one phrase in each answer.

10. Do you think people should be allowed to smoke in public places? I think ______

______

11. Do you think people should smoke in restaurants? ______

12. How does smoking affect the rights of nonsmokers? ______

D. (13–15) What is an important right for students in your school? Does anyone misuse that right? How does the misuse affect other students' rights? Write at least three complete sentences. Use at least two phrases in each sentence.

______

______

______

______

Name ______________________ Date ______________

82 What's a Compound Sentence?

Two Independent Clauses Joined by *And*, *But*, or *Or*

The words **and**, **but**, and **or** are conjunctions. They join the two clauses in a **compound sentence**. A comma (**,**) comes before the conjunction.

- Use **and** to join similar ideas.

The Bill of Rights lists people's rights. It protects people's rights.	**The Bill of Rights lists people's rights, and it protects people's rights.**

- Use **but** to join different ideas.

All people have the same rights. Some people abuse them.	**All people have the same rights, but some people abuse them.**

- Use **or** to show a choice.

People can respect those rights. They can abuse them.	**People can respect those rights, or they can abuse them.**

Try It

A. **(1–4) Use and, but, or or to combine each pair of sentences.**

Possible responses:

People have the right to a speedy trial, and the right includes trial by jury. There are witnesses against the suspect, but there are witnesses in his favor, too. A suspect has a right to a lawyer, but the suspect can waive that right. Would you represent yourself, or would you rather have a lawyer represent you?

Proofreader's Marks

Add text:

People have rights, and they have duties.

Do not capitalize:

A lawyer can help.

See all Proofreader's Marks on page ix.

B. **These compound sentences are missing and, but, or or. Edit the sentences to fix the mistakes.** Possible responses:

5. Mr. Newton is suspected of a crime and he is in custody.

6. He can defend himself or he can hire a lawyer.

7. He wants a lawyer but he can't afford one.

8. Suspects have the right to a lawyer and the state must find them one.

Write It

C. Complete each compound sentence about people's rights.

9. The Bill of Rights lists people's rights, and ______________________________
______________________________.

10. ______________________________
______________________________, but sometimes they are innocent.

11. In the United States, are people innocent until proven guilty, or ______________
______________________________.

D. (12–16) The Bill of Rights includes the right to free speech, the freedom of religion, and freedom of the press. Write at least five compound sentences to tell what you think about one or all of these rights. Use **and**, **but**, and **or**.

____
____
____
____
____
____

Edit It

E. (17–20) Edit the newspaper article. Fix the four mistakes in compound sentences. Possible responses:

Mr. Newton Is Arrested

The police have suspected Mr. John Newton of stealing money, and yesterday he was arrested. Mr. Newton says he is innocent, but he can't prove his innocence. Luckily for Mr. Newton, he is considered innocent until proven guilty. Mr. Newton has a right to a lawyer, and he has already hired Attorney Justin Green. Attorney Green will win the case for Mr. Newton, or he will lose it. Then Mr. Newton will be declared innocent, or Mr. Newton will go to jail.

Proofreader's Marks

Add text:	The Bill of Rights has 10 amendments.
Add a comma:	I have rights, and so do you.
Do not capitalize:	I am glad that we have rights.

Name ______________________ Date ____________

83 What's a Run-on Sentence?

A Sentence That Goes On and On

- To fix a run-on sentence, break it into shorter sentences or rearrange words to express the same idea.

  Run On: Rosa Parks sat on the bus **and** the bus driver told her to give her seat to a white person **and** she did not.

  Better: Rosa Parks sat on the bus. The bus driver told her to give her seat to a white person, but she refused.

- Avoid connecting too many phrases and clauses with commas. Create shorter, more understandable sentences.

  Run On: Rosa Parks was arrested **and** she was fined **and** she became an inspiration to people all over the country.

  Better: Rosa Parks was arrested and fined. However, her action inspired people all over the country.

Try It

Proofreader's Marks

Add a comma:	I learn about Rosa, and so do you.
Delete:	Rosa did not ~~not~~ get up.
Do not capitalize:	Rosa was on the /Bus.
Capitalize:	rosa was on the bus.

See all Proofreader's Marks on page ix.

A. Edit these run-on sentences. Break them into shorter sentences.

Possible responses:

1. On December 1, 1955, Rosa Parks was arrested. ~~and~~ Her trial was on December 5, and she was fined for not giving up her seat.
2. On December 4, 1955, people got together. ~~and~~ They planned the Montgomery Bus Boycott. ~~and~~ They wanted the boycott to last for one day on ~~and that day was~~ December 5.
3. People boycotted the buses in Montgomery, Alabama, and the boycott was successful. ~~and~~ The people continued to boycott the buses ~~and the boycott lasted~~ for 382 days.
4. The boycott was a protest against ~~and it protested~~ the segregation on buses in Montgomery. ~~and~~ It led to a Supreme Court ruling. ~~and~~ The ruling made segregation on buses illegal.
5. Rosa Parks stood up for her rights. ~~and~~ Her action led to the boycott, and the boycott helped other people stand up for their rights. ~~and~~ They all worked together for change.

B. **Rewrite each run-on sentence. Break it into shorter sentences and rearrange the words.** Possible responses:

6. In the 1880s, Charles Cunningham Boycott lived in Ireland and farmers asked if they could pay him less rent and Boycott said no and no one would work for him and no one would sell goods to him and no one would deliver his letters.

   In the 1880s, Charles Cunningham Boycott lived in Ireland. Farmers asked if they could pay him less rent, and Boycott said no. No one would work for him, sell goods to him, or deliver his letters.

7. Finally, Boycott had to bring in outside workers to harvest his crops and soldiers had to protect them and Boycott's name became a word and by 1897 it was part of the English language and it still is used today and it still has the same meaning.

   Finally, Boycott had to bring in outsider workers to harvest his crops, and soldiers had to protect them. By 1897, Boycott's name was a word used in the English language. It still has the same meaning today.

Write It

C. **Complete each sentence to tell about protests. Then reread your sentences to check for and fix run-ons.**

8. A boycott is ________________.

9. People boycott something to ________________
________________.

10. It is important to protest to ________________.

D. **(11–15) Rosa Parks stood up for her right to sit on the bus. Then people boycotted the buses. What is a cause you would stand up for? What would you do? Write at least five sentences. Then reread your sentences to check for and fix run-ons.**

____

____

____

____

____

Name ______________________ Date ______________

84 What's Another Kind of Compound Sentence?

Two Independent Clauses Joined by a Semicolon or a Conjunctive Adverb.

One way to form a compound sentence is to use a conjunction like **and, but,** or **or**. Here are two more ways to form compound sentences:

- Independent clauses can be joined without a conjunction by simply placing a **semicolon** between the clauses.

  Oil and coal are limited resources; it's time to switch to renewables.
  Recycling makes a difference; kids can help.

- You can also connect clauses with a conjunctive adverb such as **however, meanwhile, therefore,** or **thus**. Place a **semicolon** before the conjunctive adverb and a **comma** after it.

  Earth's resources are being depleted; **consequently,** many young people are working to preserve them.

Some Conjunctive Adverbs
also
consequently
furthermore
however
meanwhile
moreover
nevertheless
otherwise
still
therefore
thus

Try It

A. Use a semicolon or a conjunctive adverb to combine each pair of sentences.

Possible responses:

1. We need to reduce global warming. The oceans could rise by 7 to 23 inches in this century. We need to reduce global warming; otherwise, the oceans could rise by 7 to 23 inches in this century.

2. Some scientists claim that over half Earth's original oil supply has been used. Other scientists disagree. Some scientists claim that over half Earth's original oil supply has been used; however, other scientists disagree.

3. Earth's resources are being depleted or polluted. The clock is ticking. Earth's reserves are being depleted or polluted; the clock is ticking.

Write It

B. **Use each clause below in a compound sentence. Write the sentence. Combine the clauses with a conjunctive adverb.** Possible responses:

4. Recycling can help preserve resources Recycling can help preserve resources; however, more needs to be done.

5. Students at our school are taking responsibility Students at our school are taking responsibility; therefore, we have set up recycling bins for paper, plastic, and cans.

6. Petroleum reserves get smaller every day Petroleum reserves get smaller every day; meanwhile, people keep driving cars.

C. (7–9) **What responsibility can you take to protect or reserve Earth's resources? Write at least three compound sentences telling what you can do. Combine the clauses with a semicolon or conjunctive adverb.**

Edit It

Proofreader's Marks

Add Punctuation:

The students put up posters; meanwhile, the teachers made announcements.

See all Proofreader's Marks on page ix.

D. **Edit these sentences. Use correct punctuation.**

10. Recycling bins are all over; nevertheless, some kids ignore them.

11. We want more kids to recycle; thus, we put up posters.

12. The posters didn't make a big difference; they did help a little.

13. We made announcements; also, we offered rewards.

14. A few kids don't seem to care; still, most of us act responsibly.

Name ______________________________ Date ______________

85 Use Compound Sentences

Remember: A compound sentence includes two independent clauses joined by **and**, **but**, or **or**.

- Clauses may be joined by **and, but** or **or**. Use **and** to join like ideas. Use **but** to join different ideas. Use **or** to show a choice.

  Cars use the road, **and** bicycles do, too. You need a license to drive, **but** you don't need a license to ride a bike. Would you rather drive your car, **or** do you want to ride your bike?

- Clauses may also be joined by a semicolon, or with a semicolon, conjunctive adverb, and comma.

  Bikes don't have the right of way on trails**;** horses do.

  You have to yield to horses**; otherwise,** they might buck.

Try It

A. Use **and**, **or**, or **however**, to turn each pair of sentences into a compound sentence.

Possible responses:

1. In my state, pedestrians in crosswalks have the right of way, and cars have to stop.
2. Pedestrians walk facing traffic; however, riders ride in the same direction as traffic.
3. Do bicyclists have to follow the rules of the road, or can they ride against the traffic?

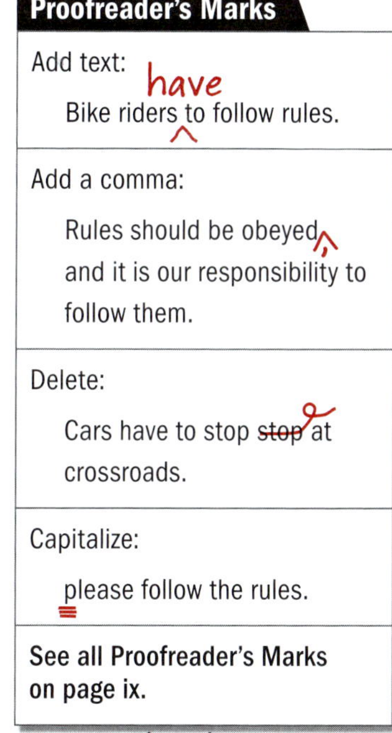

B. Edit these run-on sentences. When possible, use compound sentences.

Possible responses:

4. Dad was driving, and he didn't stop for a pedestrian in the crosswalk. He got a ticket, and he has to pay a fine.
5. Rita rides her bike to work. Sometimes she doesn't ride in the bike lane, and she got a ticket for riding the wrong way on a one-way street.
6. People use the bike path for walking, running, riding bikes, and roller blading. Everyone has to follow the bike-path rules, or no one is safe.

Write It

C. **Write compound sentences to answer the questions. Use a conjunction, a conjunctive adverb, or just a semicolon.**

7. Why is it important to know the rules of the road? ______________________________

____

8. What rules of the road do you think are most important? ______________________________

____

9. What should happen when people don't respect other people's rights to use the road?

____

D. **(10–12) Do you think it is better to walk, drive, or ride a bike to school or work? Write at least three compound sentences to explain your opinion. Then reread your sentences to check for and fix any run-ons.**

____

____

____

____

Edit It

E. **(13–15) Edit this journal entry. Fix one run-on sentence. Create two compound sentences.** Possible responses:

September 10

Today, I was late for work. and I was in a rush, and I drove too fast. and A police officer saw me, stopped me, and gave me a ticket. I broke the rules of the road, and I got punished. I'm not happy, but I learned my lesson about safe driving. It's important to respect everyone's right to be safe on the road.

Proofreader's Marks

Add text:
I drove to work.

Add a comma:
Drivers must drive safely, or they will be stopped.

Delete:
Rules of the road ~~are~~ are important.

Capitalize:
please follow the rules of the road.

Name ______________________ Date ______________

86 What's a Complex Sentence?

A Sentence with Two Kinds of Clauses

- A clause has a **subject** and a **verb**. An **independent clause** can stand alone as a sentence.

  Service organizations help people around the world.
  independent clause

- A **dependent clause** also has a subject and a verb, but it cannot stand alone.

  when people need help
  dependent clause

- You can "hook" the dependent clause to an independent clause to form a complete sentence. The new sentence is called a **complex sentence.**

  Service organizations help people around the world **when people need** help.
  independent clause — dependent clause

Try It

A. Draw a line from each independent clause to a dependent clause. There is more than one correct answer. Possible responses:

1. In some countries people cannot grow crops — when there is a drought.
2. There is not enough water — if it doesn't rain.
3. People do not have enough to eat — because they cannot grow their food.
4. Service organizations try to help — because they don't want people to suffer.
5. Some organizations have food drives — because they want to prevent starvation.
6. Sometimes volunteers travel to faraway places — if people there need their help.

B. Write an independent clause to make each dependent clause into a complete sentence.

Possible responses:

7. I volunteer in a service organization overseas because I want to help people grow food.

8. Some children don't get enough to eat if their village doesn't have enough food.

9. I had never seen starving children before I lived in this village.

10. I asked my friends from home to send donations after I got here.

11. The children are really happy when the packages arrive.

12. I am happy here because I am helping other people survive.

Write It

C. Make each independent clause into a complex sentence. Add a dependent clause.

13. People volunteer in service organizations ______________________________ .

14. It is important to volunteer ______________________________ .

15. Some people don't have enough to eat ______________________________ .

16. I help out ______________________________ .

D. (17–20) Do you think having enough food to eat is a basic human right? Write at least four complex sentences to explain your opinion.

____

____

____

____

____

Name ______________________ Date ____________

87 Can a Clause Act Like an Adverb?

Yes, and It Often Tells When or Why.

- A **complex sentence** has one independent clause and one dependent clause.

  People work because they need to earn a living.
  independent clause (People work) — dependent clause (because they need to earn a living.)

- When the **dependent clause** acts like an adverb, it begins with a **subordinating conjunction**. The conjunction shows how the two clauses are related.

Tells When:	**After I get out of college**, I will get a job.
Tells Why:	I will work **because I will need to support myself**.
Tells What May Happen:	**If I get a good job,** I will be happy.

- **Conjunctions include:** after, because, if, before, when, whenever, while, until, since, unless, although, where

Try It

A. Create a complex sentence. Add a clause that begins with a subordinating conjunction. Possible responses:

1. Everyone should have the right to earn a living because most people need money to survive.
2. When I apply for jobs, people consider my training and experience.
3. They judge me on my experience although they consider my appearance, too.
4. Some programs help people find jobs when the people need more training.
5. If the people work hard and learn a lot, there are jobs waiting for them at the end of the program.
6. After they begin to work, people are proud to be supporting themselves.

B. **Fix these complex sentences. Add subordinating conjunctions.**

Possible responses:

7. People have a right to safety ^while they are at work.

8. ^Before ~~T~~there were labor laws, many people worked in sweatshops.

9. Conditions were not safe in the sweatshops ^where people were working.

10. The government made laws ^because the working conditions were so unsafe.

11. ^After ~~P~~people formed unions, the unions fought for safer workplaces, too.

12. ^Although ~~T~~there aren't as many sweatshops in the United States today, there are still sweatshops in countries around the world.

13. Organizations try to protect workers' rights ^because everyone has the right to safety at work.

Proofreader's Marks

Do not capitalize:

Sweatshops were not ~~S~~afe.

Add text:

Sweatshops were not ^safe.

See all Proofreader's Marks on page ix.

Write It

C. **Answer each question about the right to work. Use complex sentences.**

14. When do you think kids should have the right to work? ____________________

____

15. Why do you think kids should have the right to work? ____________________

____

16. Do you work? Why or why not? ____________________

____

D. **(17–20) Do you think it is okay to have sweatshops? Do you think labor laws should protect workers' rights? Write at least four complex sentences to tell what you think about safety in the workplace.**

____

____

____

____

____

____

Name ______________________ Date ____________

88 Can a Clause Act Like an Adjective?

Yes, and It Often Begins with *Who*, *That*, or *Which*.

- A **complex sentence** has one independent clause and one dependent clause.

  I have school books that help me learn important information.
  (independent clause: I have school books; dependent clause: that help me learn important information)

- Some **dependent clauses** act like adjectives and tell more about nouns. They begin with a **relative pronoun**.

  1. Use **who** to tell about people. **2.** Use **that** for things or people.

  3. Use **which** for things.

- Place an **adjective clause** right after the noun it describes.

  Some children **who go to school** don't have school books.

  I am a member of an organization **that gets school supplies for children.**

Try It

A. Write adjective clauses to make complex sentences. Possible responses:

1. There are many people who donate school supplies to children in need.

2. I work for a company that collects backpacks to donate.

3. I shop at a store that donates paper and pencils.

4. Some people who live in my community collect books and supplies to send.

B. (5–8) Write adjective clauses to make complex sentences to complete the paragraph about a school that has an adopt-a-school program. Possible responses:

My school has an adopt-a-school program. It donates supplies to a school that needs school supplies. Many children who go to the other school can't afford to buy supplies. My school asks businesses that are in our community to donate supplies to the program. My school also asks the students who go to school here to recycle school supplies, like backpacks, to donate.

Write It

C. **Write complex sentences to tell how the people or things named in parentheses could help provide school books or supplies. Use an adjective clause in each sentence.**

9. (service organization) ______________________________

____

10. (student volunteer) ______________________________

____

11. (local business or store) ______________________________

____

D. **(12–15) Why is it important for students to have books and supplies? What can you do to help? Write at least four complex sentences with adjective clauses.**

____

____

____

____

Edit It

E. **(16–20) Edit the journal entry. Add five relative pronouns.**

June 29

I have a friend who couldn't afford school supplies when she went to elementary school. Now, she is an adult. She has started a program ^that donates supplies to children in need. She works for a store ^that helps her. The person ^who manages the store is a big help. The store has a big bucket ^that shoppers can fill with donated supplies, ^which are sent to relief organizations.

Proofreader's Marks

Add text:

I know a student ^who needs supplies.

See all Proofreader's Marks on page ix.

Name ______________________ Date ______________

89 What's a Compound-Complex Sentence?

It's Complicated.

- A **compound-complex sentence** has two or more independent clauses and one or more dependent clauses.

  You have customs, and I have different customs that are important to me.
  (You have customs — independent clause; I have different customs — independent clause; that are important to me — dependent clause)

  Because we have rights, I can have my beliefs, and you can have yours.
  (Because we have rights — dependent clause; I can have my beliefs — independent clause; you can have yours — independent clause)

Try It

A. Write an independent clause to change each complex sentence into a compound-complex sentence. Possible responses:

The Bill of Rights, which is part of the Constitution, lists some of our rights, and freedom of religion is one of them. People who believe in their customs have that right, but I can still believe in my customs, too. Freedom of speech, which is also a right in the Bill of Rights, lets me speak about my beliefs, but you don't have to agree with me. Rights that protect our freedom are important, and I'm glad to live in a country that has those rights.

B. Write a dependent clause to change each compound sentence into a compound-complex sentence. Possible responses:

People who live in some countries don't have freedom of speech, but people in this country do. I can say what I believe, and you can have beliefs that are different from mine. Although I might disagree with you, you can have your beliefs, and I can have mine. Because we have this right, our country is special, and I'm glad to live in it.

Write It

C. Write compound-complex sentences to tell about customs that are important to you.

9. One important custom that ______________ is ______________, and ______________
____.

10. It is important because ______________________________, but ______________
____.

11. When ______________, I ______________, or ______________________
____.

D. (12–15) Write at least four compound-complex sentences to tell about different customs or beliefs that people you know have.

____

____

____

____

____

____

Edit It

E. (16–20) Edit this letter. Make the five corrections to compound-complex sentences.

Dear Aunt Mary,

Today, we read the Bill of Rights, and I learned about some rights ^that are guaranteed in the Constitution. The rights are important ^because they protect us, ^and they give us freedoms. A right ^that guarantees free speech is important. Maybe one day everyone ^who lives anywhere in the world will have equal rights, but I'm not sure that everyone has equal rights today.

Love,

Dan

Proofreader's Marks

Add text:

You have rights, ^and I have rights ^because we live in this country.

See all Proofreader's Marks on page ix.

Name ______________________ Date ____________

90 Use Complex Sentences

Remember: When you use a variety of sentences, your writing is more interesting.

Expand a simple sentence to a **complex sentence**.

- Add an **adjective clause** to tell more about a noun. Use a **relative pronoun** (that, which, who).

  People learn about other countries.

  People **who travel** learn about other countries.

- Add an **adverb clause** to tell more about an action. Use a **subordinating conjunction** (after, although, because, if, when).

  They meet people from different parts of the world.

  When people travel, they meet people from different parts of the world.

Try It

A. Create a complex sentence by adding an adjective clause. Possible responses:

1. I am a volunteer in a service organization that sends volunteers all around the world.
2. I travel to villages that are poor and underprivileged.
3. People who live in the villages don't always have the rights or freedoms that I have.

B. Create a complex sentence by adding an adverb clause. Possible responses:

4. When I travel, I see how other people live.
5. I like to visit different places because I want to see the whole world.
6. If I could, I would change the world to make it a better place for everyone.

Write It

C. **Answer the questions with complex sentences. Include adjective and adverb phrases.**

7. How can traveling help you learn about human rights around the world? ______________

____

8. Where might you find people with fewer rights or privileges than you have? ______________

____

9. What can you do to help promote human rights around the world? ______________

____

D. **(10–11) Where would you like to travel to? Why? Write at least two complex sentences about a trip you would like to take. Use at least one adjective clause and one adverb clause.**

____

____

____

____

Edit It

E. **(12–15) Edit this journal entry. Add two adjective clauses and two adverb clauses to make the paragraph more interesting.** Possible responses:

May 29

Today, I visited a village that has hungry people in it. This was a whole new experience for me. I met people ^who don't have enough to eat^. They don't have enough food ^because their parents can't afford to buy it^. This made me feel very sad. ^When I get back home,^ I'm going to organize a food and clothing drive. My community can work towards making life easier for people ^who are not as fortunate as we are.^

Proofreader's Marks

Add text: It is sad to see people ^who are hungry^.

See all Proofreader's Marks on page ix.

Name ______________________ Date ____________

Edit and Proofread

Capitalize the Names of Days, Months, and Holidays

- Capitalize the names of days, months, and holidays because they are proper nouns.

  On **Tuesday** evening, the town council held a meeting.

  They decided to extend the curfew to 11:00 P.M. beginning in **June**.

  Unfortunately, it won't happen in time for **Memorial Day**.

- Do not capitalize the seasons of the year because they are common nouns.

  At least we'll have a later curfew for the entire **summer**.

  The curfew will go back to 10:00 P.M. in the **fall**.

Try It

A. (1–8) Fix the eight capitalization errors in the letter. Use proofreader's marks.

Dear Mayor Williams:

I am writing to request that you consider a later curfew on Weekdays during the Summer. Many high school students, myself included, work full-time jobs from monday through friday when school is out. The early weekday curfew means we cannot be scheduled to work the later shift because we won't get home in time. It also means we can't work extra hours on independence day or labor day to earn time-and-a-half. Allowing teenagers to stay out an hour later would give us many more employment opportunities—something that would definitely keep us out of trouble. Please consider this request during the next council meeting.

Sincerely,

Sam Eckman

Proofreader's Marks

Capitalize:

Curfew is 11:00 P.M. on friday and saturday nights.

Do not capitalize:

I don't like to stay out late in the Winter.

See all Proofreader's Marks on page ix.

Name ______________________________ Date ______________

Use Commas with Introductory Phrases and Clauses

- Place a comma at the end of an introductory clause. An **introductory clause** is a dependent clause that provides background information for the main part of the sentence.

  Because you came home before curfew, you will be rewarded.

- Place a comma at the end of an introductory phrase. An **introductory phrase** also provides background information for the main part of the sentence, but it doesn't have both a subject and a verb.

  After getting home by curfew, I was rewarded.

  The next day, my parents extended my curfew.

Try It

Proofreader's Marks

Add a comma:

By tomorrow evening I will know if I have the job.

A. Edit each sentence. Add a comma where necessary. Use proofreader's marks.

9. If we volunteer at the food pantry we will have to be out past curfew.

10. As a law-abiding citizen I am against that idea.

11. So that we don't break curfew we could always leave ten minutes early.

12. Since we would be volunteers leaving a little early would probably be OK.

B. Complete each sentence by adding an introductory clause or phrase. Be sure to use commas correctly.

13. ______________________________ I tried to make it home before 10:30.

14. ______________________________ I would be in big trouble with my parents.

15. ______________________________ my ride came.

16. ______________________________ I was able to make it home on time.

Name ______________________ Date ______________

Edit and Proofread

Use Precise Language

- Substitute a word or phrase with a word or phrase that is more specific.
  Our town has **a curfew.**
  Our town has **a curfew of 10:00 P.M. on weekdays and 11:00 P.M. on weekends.**
- Replace words such as **few**, **many**, and **some** with specific amounts.
  A bunch of teens were caught breaking curfew last year.
  Fifty-six teens were caught breaking curfew last year.
- Add a word or phrase to provide more information about another word.
  Curfews are **wrong.**
  Curfews are **wrong because they are a form of discrimination against young people.**

Try It

A. Rewrite each sentence. Replace the underlined word or phrase with more precise language or add more precise language to describe it.

17. Last night, there was a big event at South Park.

____

18. Some kids in town were ticketed for staying out past curfew.

____

19. The tickets cost them each a lot of money.

____

20. They also had to perform some community service.

____

21. The kids' names were printed in the newspaper.

____

22. From then on, the kids made sure they were home early.

____

Name ______________________ Date ______________

Build Effective Sentences

- When joining two sentences with a **subordinating conjunction**, make sure the conjunction goes with the sentence that supports the main sentence.

  Incorrect: If you are breaking the law, you stay out after curfew.

  Correct: If you stay out after curfew, you are breaking the law.

- When combining sentences, keep elements of the new sentence parallel in form. This means they should have the same word pattern.

  Incorrect: I like **going out** with friends and **to work** late.

  Correct: I like **going out** with friends and **working late**.

Subordinating Conjunctions
before, when (to show time)
because, so (to show cause and effect)
although, even though (to show opposition)
if, unless (to show a condition)

Try It

A. Rewrite each sentence. Correct the placement of the subordinating conjunction or make sentence parts parallel in form. Possible responses:

23. Many teens have good reasons for being out after curfew, such as babysitting and to study with friends.

Many teens have good reasons for being out after curfew, such as babysitting and studying with friends.

24. Some teens are causing trouble late at night because the curfew applies to all teens.

Because some teens are causing trouble late at night, the curfew applies to all teens.

25. Since it wouldn't reduce crime very much, a curfew would not apply to adults.

Since a curfew would not apply to adults, it wouldn't reduce crime very much.

Name ______________________ Date __________

91 Why Do Verbs Have So Many Forms?

Because They Change to Show When an Action Happens

The tense of a verb shows when an action happens.

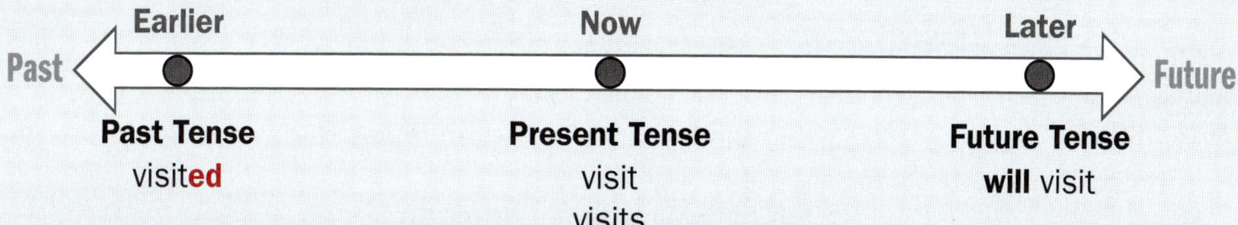

- **Present tense** verbs tell about actions that happen now or on a regular basis.

  My family and I often **visit** Washington, D.C. We **see** the monuments there.

- **Past tense** verbs tell about an action that already happened.
  Add **-ed** to show the past, or use the correct form of an irregular verb.

  We **visited** the Lincoln Memorial yesterday. We **saw** the White House, too.

Present Tense	am, is	are	have, has	go, goes	see, sees
Past Tense	was	were	had	went	saw

- **Future tense** verbs tell about actions that haven't happened yet.

  We **will visit** the Vietnam Veterans Memorial tomorrow. We **will see** all the names.

Try It

A. Describe the visit. Rewrite each sentence, changing the verb to the past tense.

1. The monuments in Washington, D.C., fill me with awe and respect. The monuments in Washington, D.C., filled me with awe and respect.
2. The Lincoln Memorial impresses me the most. The Lincoln Memorial impressed me the most.
3. The statue of Lincoln is awesome. The statue of Lincoln was awesome.
4. The memorial has a message of freedom for us all. The memorial had a message of freedom for us all.

B. **Complete each sentence. Write the correct tense of the verb in parentheses.**

5. Right now we ___are___ at the Vietnam Veterans Memorial. **(be)**

6. It ___is___ a black granite wall that shows the names of soldiers. **(be)**

7. The soldiers ___died___ a long time ago in the Vietnam War. **(die)**

8. Maya Ying Lin ___designed___ the memorial in 1981. **(design)**

9. My mom first ___saw___ the wall in 1982 when it was dedicated. **(see)**

10. Now I ___stand___ before the wall with her. **(stand)**

11. Maybe one day I ___will bring___ my own children here. **(bring)**

12. If I do, they probably ___will have___ the same feelings of awe and respect that I have. **(have)**

Write It

C. **Complete each sentence about a memorial you have seen or read about. Use the correct verb tense in each sentence.**

13. In the past, I ______________________________

______________________________.

14. Right now, I ______________________________

______________________________.

15. Someday soon, I ______________________________

______________________________.

D. (16–20) **What places give you a sense of awe and respect? Write at least five sentences. Use the past, present, and future tense at least one time each.**

____

____

____

____

____

____

Name ______________________ Date ____________

92 What If An Action Happened But You're Not Sure When?

Use the Present Perfect Tense to Tell About It.

- If you know when an action happened in the past, use a **past tense** verb.

  Yesterday, I **dressed** in my best suit.

- If you're not sure when a past action happened, use a verb in the **present perfect tense**.

  I **have dressed** in my best suit before.

- To form the present perfect, use the helping verb **have** or **has** plus the **past participle** of the main verb. For regular verbs, the past participle ends in **-ed**.

Verb	Past Tense	Past Participle
celebrate	celebrated	celebrated
shop	shopped	shopped
try	tried	tried

Try It

A. Complete each sentence. Write the correct tense of the verb.

1. Yesterday, I ___interviewed___ for a job.
   interviewed / have interviewed
2. I ___have tried___ to get a job many times this month.
   tried / have tried
3. I really ___wanted___ to get this particular job yesterday.
   wanted / have wanted
4. That's why yesterday I ___dressed___ in my best suit.
   dressed / have dressed
5. My dad says that dressing well ___has helped___ him find a good job.
   helped / has helped

B. **Complete each sentence. Write the past or present perfect tense of the verb in parentheses.**

6. Last weekend, I shopped for a fancy new dress. **(shop)**

7. I have hated wearing fancy dresses so far. **(hate)**

8. Now, I wanted to buy something really nice. **(want)**

9. Yesterday, my parents and I traveled to my grandparents' house. **(travel)**

10. We planned to surprise my grandparents. **(plan)**

11. In the evening, we celebrated their 50th wedding anniversary. **(celebrate)**

12. I have respected my grandparents since I was very young. **(respect)**

13. For the party, I dressed in my fancy new dress to show that respect. **(dress)**

Write It

C. **Answer each question about how you dress. Use the present perfect tense.**

14. Recently, what have you changed about what you wear? ______________________

____

15. What kind of clothes have you most liked to wear? ______________________

____

16. Have you always dressed the same for school as you have for special occasions? Why or why not? ______________________

____

D. (17–20) **When have you dressed up to show respect? Write at least four sentences. Use the present perfect tense.**

____

____

____

____

____

Name ______________________________ Date ______________

93 What If a Past Action Is Still Going On?

Then Use the Present Perfect Tense.

- Use the **present perfect tense** to show that an action began in the past and may still be happening.

  My family **has recycled** for years. (We are still recycling.)

  We **have tried** to respect the environment. (We are still trying to respect it.)

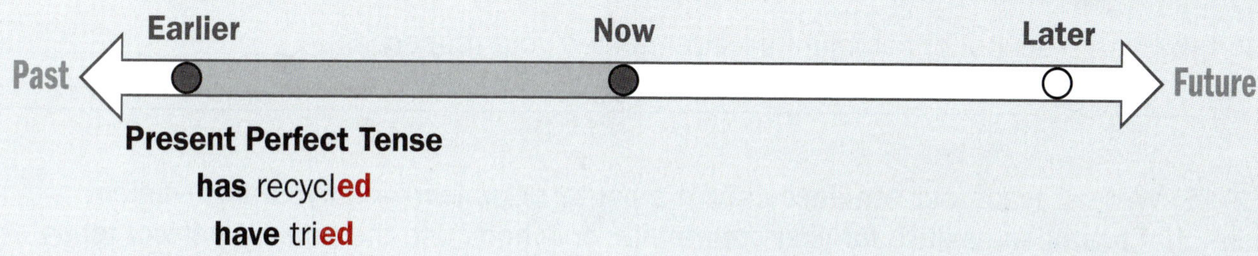

- A verb in the present perfect tense uses the helping verb **have** or **has** plus the **past participle** of the main verb. For regular verbs, the past participle ends in **-ed**.

Try It

A. **Complete each sentence. Write the present perfect form of the verb in parentheses.**

1. I ___have admired___ our mayor for a long time. **(admire)**
2. She ___has supported___ important causes in our city. **(support)**
3. Recently, the mayor ___has started___ a recycling project. **(start)**
4. We ___have experienced___ a decrease in garbage since the project began. **(experience)**

B. **(5–8) Complete each sentence with a verb in the present perfect. Choose from the verbs in the box.** Possible responses:

endorse	plant	work	vote

The mayor ___has worked___ hard to make our city better. She ___has endorsed___ my school's Beautify the City project. As a result, the students at my school ___have planted___ flowers in city parks. My parents ___have voted___ for the mayor in the past, and they will again.

Write It

C. Answer the questions about your community. Use the present perfect tense.

9. How have you helped make your community a better place to live? I ______

______

10. What are some causes that you have supported? ______

______

11. How has a school or community leader gained your respect? ______

______

D. (12–15) Write at least four sentences about a cause or project—and your involvement in it—that has been positive for your community or school. Use the present perfect tense.

______

______

______

______

______

Edit It

E. (16–20) Edit the news story. Fix the five mistakes with present perfect verbs.

Mayor Jones Makes the Grade

Mayor Kristen Jones has gained the respect of the whole community. For years, she ~~have~~ has worked tirelessly to make this city a better place to live. Mayor Jones has ~~help~~ helped beautify the city with her monthly clean-up day. People ~~has pitch~~ have pitched in to help pick up garbage from neighborhood streets. They ~~has~~ have worked together. We are lucky to have people like Mayor Jones running our city. These amazing people have ~~inspire~~ inspired us all.

Proofreader's Marks

Add text:

Mrs. Jones has decided to run for mayor again.

Change text:

She ~~have ask~~ has asked for our help.

See all Proofreader's Marks on page ix.

Name ______________________ Date ____________

94 Do All Past Participles End in *-ed*?

No, Irregular Verbs have Special Forms.

- Past participles of irregular verbs have a completely new spelling.

	Verb	Past Tense	Past Participle
Forms of *Be*	am, is	was	been
	are	were	been
	give	gave	given
	go	went	gone
	see	saw	seen

- Use **has** or **have** plus the past participle to form the **present perfect tense**.
  My family **has been** to Russia. We **have seen** where my dad grew up.

Try It

A. **Complete each sentence. Write the present perfect form of the verb in parentheses.**

1. I have gone to Russia several times. **(go)**
2. My brothers and sisters have been there, too. **(be)**
3. Each time, our relatives there have given us a tour. **(give)**
4. We have seen what life in Russia was like for Grandma. **(see)**

B. **Rewrite each sentence in the present perfect tense.**

5. Grandma saw a lot of hard times. Grandma has seen a lot of hard times.
6. She gave up many things. She has given up many things.
7. We were lucky as a result. We have been lucky as a result.

Write It

C. Answer the questions about visiting relatives. Use the present perfect tense.

8. What relative have you visited recently? I ______________________________.

9. What has the relative done that you will never have to do? ______________________________

____

10. What have you learned about the relative that made you respectful? ______________________________

____

11. What have you given to your relative in return? ______________________________

____

D. (12–15) Write at least four sentences about how your parents or grandparents have changed your life to make it better than theirs was. Use the present perfect tense.

____

____

____

____

Edit It

E. (16–20) Edit this letter. Fix the five mistakes with present perfect verbs.

Dear Uncle Toni,

We are having a great trip. So far, we ^have gone up the mountain road three times to visit the village where Grandma lived. Best of all, we ^have seen the house she grew up in. The man who lives there now ~~have~~ ^has been very kind to us. He ~~give~~ ^has given us an open invitation to come back anytime.

I can't wait to show you my photos. It ~~have~~ ^has been the trip of a lifetime!

Love,

Carlos

Proofreader's Marks

Add text:

I ^have seen the village.

Change text:

This trip ~~have~~ ^has given me more respect for Grandma.

See all Proofreader's Marks on page ix.

Name ______________________ Date ____________

95 Verbs in the Present Perfect Tense

Remember: Use **have** or **has** plus the past participle of a verb to form the present perfect tense.

- The past participle of a **regular verb** ends in **-ed**.
  Dad **has trained** to run in the marathon. **(train + -ed)**
  We **have realized** that he will finish no matter what. **(realize [– e] + -ed)**
- The past participle of an **irregular verb** has a completely new spelling.

Verb	Past Participle
be	been
come	come
get	got or gotten

Verb	Past Participle
see	seen
show	shown
take	taken

Try It

A. **Complete each sentence. Write the present perfect tense of the verb in parentheses.**

1. My dad ___has shown___ a lot of courage. **(show)**
2. He ___has survived___ many surgeries. **(survive)**
3. We ___have seen___ him get stronger each time. **(see)**
4. Marathons always ___have been___ a hobby of his. **(be)**
5. That's why he ___has decided___ to participate in this marathon. **(decide)**

B. **Rewrite each sentence in the present perfect tense.**

6. We come to see Dad race. We have come to see Dad race.
7. He races in his wheelchair. He has raced in his wheelchair.
8. It takes him a long time to finish. It has taken him a long time to finish.

C. Complete each sentence about how Dad and his family have felt after each race. Use the present perfect tense.

9. My dad ____
____.

10. I ____
____.

11. My whole family ____
____.

D. (12–15) Think of a person you have respected. Why have you respect that person? Write at least four sentences. Use the present perfect tense.

____
____
____
____
____

E. (16–20) Edit this journal entry. Fix the five mistakes in present perfect verb forms.

June 23

Dad has completed his first marathon in a wheelchair. He has ~~showed~~ shown us all how to be courageous. I have seen Dad bounce back after every surgery. He has ~~hold~~ held his head up high. My respect for him ~~have~~ has grown every year. I ~~has decide~~ have decided to be more like him in the future. I'm so glad to have Dad for my dad.

Proofreader's Marks

Add text:
I have seen him race.

Change text:
Dad ~~have~~ has faced many challenges.

See all Proofreader's Marks on page ix.

Name ______________________________ Date ______________

96 How Do You Show Which Past Action Happened First?

Use the Past Perfect Tense.

- Use the **past tense** of a verb to tell about an action that was completed in the past.
  My older brother **played** tennis with me.
- If you want to show that one past action happened before another, use the **past perfect tense** for the action that happened first.
  He **had won** two tennis tournaments by the time he **graduated** from high school.

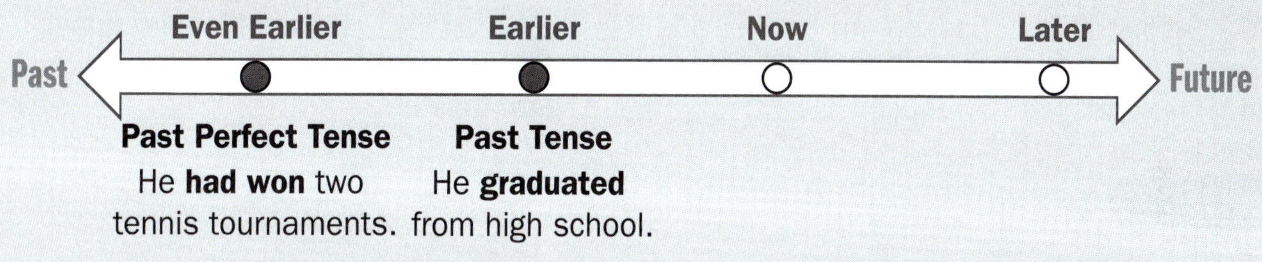

Past Perfect Tense
He **had won** two tennis tournaments.

Past Tense
He **graduated** from high school.

- To form the **past perfect tense**, use **had** plus the **past participle** of the main verb.
  I **missed** him after he **had been** at college for a while.

Try It

A. **Complete each sentence with the past perfect form of the verb in parentheses.**

1. On the day my brother left for college, I realized I ___had taken___ him for granted. **(take)**
2. I never ___had been___ the only child at home before. **(be)**
3. Sure, he ___had teased___ me, but now I missed that. **(tease)**
4. I even liked that we ___had shared___ a bedroom. **(share)**
5. I remembered how he ___had played___ tennis with me. **(play)**
6. I thought about how he ___had given___ me guitar lessons. **(give)**
7. Now he was gone, and everything ___had changed___. **(change)**

B. **Complete each sentence. Write the past tense or past perfect tense of the verb in parentheses.**

8. My brother had been away for two months when he ___came___ home for a visit. **(come)**

9. I already ___had gone___ to school on the day he arrived. **(go)**

10. When I ___got___ home, he had already been home for several hours. **(get)**

11. I was really happy that he ___had decided___ to visit. **(decide)**

12. My parents and I ___had planned___ a big dinner before he arrived. **(plan)**

13. Before an hour passed, my brother and I ___had played___ a set of tennis. **(play)**

14. I realized just how much I ___had missed___ him. **(miss)**

Write It

C. **Complete each sentence about something else the two siblings did together before the older brother went back to school. Use past and past perfect tense verbs.**

15. Before he ____________, my brother and I ____________________
____.

16. I ____________ until he ____________________
____.

17. After he ____________, I ____________________
____.

D. **(18–20) Write at least three sentences about a relationship that you have with a family member. Tell about something you did together in the past. Use the past perfect tense in each sentence.**

____
____
____
____
____

Name ______________________ Date ____________

97 How Do You Know Which Tense to Use?

Think About When the Action Happened.

- When you tell about the past, you may need to relate actions in time. First use the past tense to tell what happened.
  Maura **moved** in September.
- Then use the **past perfect tense** to tell what happened before Maura moved.
  Maura **moved** to Glendale, but she **had lived** in Springfield for many years.
- Sometimes a past action may still be going on. That's when you use the **present perfect tense**.
  Maura **has kept** the same friends for years.
  She **has stayed** in touch with her friends since she **moved**.

Try It

A. Complete each sentence. Write the correct tense of the verb.

1. Maura ____has lived____ in Glendale since September.
   lived / has lived
2. She ____grew____ up in Springfield.
   grew / has grown
3. By the time she moved, Maura ____had played____ field hockey for two seasons.
   has played / had played
4. She ____tried____ out for Glendale High School field hockey team.
   tried / has tried

B. Complete each sentence. Write the past, present perfect, or past perfect tense of the verb in parentheses.

5. By the time the season ended, Maura ____had made____ many new friends. **(make)**
6. She still ____missed____ her old friends, though. **(miss)**
7. That's why she ____got____ in touch with them before her birthday party. **(get)**
8. Last week, Maura ____invited____ her old friends and her new friends to her party. **(invite)**

Write It

C. Complete each sentence about a friend. Use the correct tense of verbs to show past actions.

9. Last week, my friend and I ____.

10. Before we did that, we ____.

11. Since then, we ____.

D. (12–15) Have you heard the expression "Make new friends, but keep the old"? Write at least four sentences about how it has related to you. Use the past tense, the present perfect tense, and the past perfect tense at least one time each.

____

____

____

____

Edit It

E. (16–20) Edit this letter. Fix the five mistakes in verb tenses.

Dear Isabella,

I'm so glad that you came to my party last week. I'm sorry that by the time you got here, we ~~ate~~ had eaten most of the cake. Well, at least we ~~have gotten~~ got to visit with each other, and that's what counts. I am learning how important it is to have good friends. My new friends here ~~be~~ have been very nice to me. They will never replace you, though. I ~~has~~ have known you for fifteen years! I have ~~learn~~ learned that good friends are the best gift of all.

Love,

Maura

Proofreader's Marks

Change text:

Maura ~~write~~ wrote to her friend last night.

See all Proofreader's Marks on page ix.

Name ______________________ Date ______________

98 When Do You Use the Future Perfect Tense?

When You Want to Relate a Future Action to a Future Time

- Sometimes an action that hasn't yet happened depends on another future event. That's when you use the **future perfect tense**.

  Soon **we will leave on our trip.** By then, I **will have made** all my plans.

  Before we go, I **will have finished** all of my work.

Future Perfect Tense
I **will have called**
Grandma and Grandpa, too.

- To form the **future perfect tense**, use **will have** plus the **past participle** of the main verb.

  Before we arrive at the ferry, we **will have driven** for five hours.

  Before we arrive on the island, we **will have been** on the ferry for two hours.

Try It

A. Complete each sentence. Write the future perfect tense of the verb in parentheses.

1. Just think: By this time tomorrow, my family and I will have boarded the ferry. **(board)**
2. The ferry will have taken us all the way to the island. **(take)**
3. It will have docked in the harbor. **(dock)**
4. Grandpa will have come to meet us at the boat. **(come)**
5. We will have eaten lunch at the fish stand. **(eat)**
6. We will have shopped at the market. **(shop)**
7. We will have stopped for fresh bread at the bakery. **(stop)**
8. By this time tomorrow, we will have arrived at our final destination, Grandma's cottage. **(arrive)**

B. Complete each sentence with a future perfect tense verb. Possible responses:

9. When this summer ends, Lisa will have spent ten summers on the island.

10. Right now, Lisa is 16. By the time she goes home, she will have turned 17.

11. She will have celebrated her birthday at a place she loves and with people she loves, too.

12. Before Lisa leaves the island, she will have sailed her boat in the bay.

13. She will have played volleyball every morning, and she will have gone swimming at the beach every afternoon.

14. She also will have made money working at her summer job.

Write It

C. Suppose Lisa will spend one day hiking on a nature trail on the island. Complete the sentences about what she will do or see. Use the future perfect tense.

15. By the end of the day, Lisa ______________________________

______________________________.

16. When she gets to the end of the trail, she ______________________________

______________________________.

17. Soon, the sun ______________________________

______________________________.

D. (18–20) What is your favorite place? What do you do there? Write at least three sentences about the place. Use the future perfect tense.

____

____

____

____

____

Name ______________________ Date ____________

99 How Are the Past Perfect and Future Perfect Tenses Alike?

They Both Show How One Action Happens Before Another.

- Use the **past perfect tense** to help your readers know that an action happened even earlier than another past action.

  By the time school got out, I **had visited** Grandma ten times.

- Use the **future perfect tense** to help your readers know that an action will happen before some other time in the future.

  By the time my vacation ends, I **will have visited** Grandma three more times.

Try It

A. Complete each sentence. Write the past perfect or future perfect tense of the verb in parentheses.

1. I remember that last weekend. When we got to Grandma's house, we could tell from the delicious smell that she <u>had prepared</u> a huge dinner for us. **(prepare)**

2. By the time the adults were finished with the main meal, my brothers, sisters, cousins, and I <u>had run</u> outside to play. **(run)**

3. After a while, we were called inside for dessert. Even though we <u>had filled</u> our plates with chicken and potatoes, we still had room for apple pie. **(fill)**

4. By the time I see Grandma again, she <u>will have settled</u> into her new life in the assisted living facility. **(settle)**

B. Complete each sentence with a past perfect or a future perfect tense verb. Possible responses:

5. Last fall, Grandma got very sick. I thought about how she <u>had kept</u> our whole family together over the years.

6. I realized now how lucky I <u>had been</u> to have her for my grandma.

7. Before she becomes too sick, I <u>will have told</u> Grandma how much I love her.

8. Before she dies, I hope that I <u>will have done</u> something special for her.

Write It

C. Complete each sentence about a family member you love and respect. Use the past perfect or future perfect tense.

9. Before I was a teenager, I ____

____.

10. Before my ________________, we always ______________________________

____.

11. Before this year is over, ________________ and I ______________________

____.

D. (12–15) Write at least four sentences about how parents and grandparents keep families together. Use the past perfect or future perfect tense in each sentence.

____

____

____

____

____

Edit It

E. (16–20) Edit this letter. Fix the five mistakes in past perfect or future perfect verbs.

Dear Grandma,

By the time you get this letter, I ^will have performed in my piano recital. This morning, I thought about how we used to play our duets. Remembering that made me sad because I know you won't be at my recital. Mom suggested I tape the recital, but I ^had decided to do that already. Before you see me again, you ^will have heard me on the tape. You ^will have imagined you were there! By then you will ^have had the chance to say whether I was good or bad! Then we can listen together during my next visit.

Love,

Zac

Proofreader's Marks

Add text:

I ^have given Grandma a tape.

See all Proofreader's Marks on page ix.

Name ________________________ Date ____________

100 Write with the Perfect Tenses

Remember: Use the present perfect, past perfect, and future perfect tenses to show how actions are related in time. Study the chart.

Tense	When Do You Use It?	Examples
Present Perfect	For actions that began in the past and are still going on	Aunt Lil **has been** my role model for years.
	For actions that happened at an unknown past time	I **have visited** her a lot.
Past Perfect	For actions completed before another past action	By the time she got her apartment, Aunt Lil **had lived** with us for two years.
Future Perfect	For actions that will happen before a future time	By the end of the month, she **will have bought** a house.

Try It

A. Complete each sentence. Write the correct perfect tense of the verb in parentheses.

1. I have known Aunt Lil my whole life. **(know)**
2. She always has served as a role model to me. **(serve)**
3. By the time she was thirty, she had finished medical school. **(finish)**
4. Next month, she will have been a doctor for thirty years. **(be)**

B. (5–8) Complete each sentence with a verb in the perfect tense. Use work, spend, and accomplish. You may need to use a verb more than once.

Aunt Lil has worked hard her whole life. By the time she was 22, she had worked her way through college. By the time she became a doctor, she had spent years working at a hospital. By the time I am her age, I hope I will have accomplished as much as she has.

Write It

C. Answer the questions. Use the present perfect, the past perfect, and the future perfect tenses.

9. What have you worked hard at? I ______________________________ .

10. What had you done before you turned fifteen? ______________________________

11. By the time you grow up, what will you have accomplished? ______________________________

D. (12–16) Who is your role model? Why has that person been a model to you? Write at least five sentences. Use the present perfect, the past perfect, and the future perfect tenses.

____

____

____

____

____

Edit It

E. (17–20) Edit this letter. Fix the four perfect tense verbs.

Dear Aunt Lil,

I have almost ~~complete~~ completed my first year of medical school. Your encouragement ~~have~~ has helped me tremendously. By the time I finish medical school, I will have learned so much. You have been there to support me the whole time. I hope that one day I will be the same kind of role model for someone else like you have been for me.

Love,

Juanita

Proofreader's Marks

Add text:
have
I had a tough semester.

Change text:
has
Aunt Lil ~~have~~ been a great role model.

See all Proofreader's Marks on page ix.

Name ______________________ Date ____________

101 Can a Verb Act Like an Adjective?

Yes, When It Is a Participle

- Verbs have **four principal parts**. For example:

Present	Present Participle	Past	Past Participle
fly	flying	flew	flown
sing	singing	sang	sung

- Sometimes a **participle** is part of a verb phrase. Sometimes, however, it acts as an adjective to describe a noun or pronoun.

In spring, the birds **are singing**. The **singing** birds make nests.

Flying, the birds sing. They **are singing**.

The **singing** birds sounds pretty. **Singing**, they fly away.

Try It

A. Combine the sentences. Move the underlined participles to tell about a noun or a pronoun in the other sentence.

1. In winter, I love to watch the snow. The snow is **falling**.
   In winter, I love to watch the falling snow.

2. After the snow stops, I skate on the pond. The pond is **frozen**.
   After the snow stops, I skate on the frozen pond.

3. I go home for hot chocolate. I am **refreshed**.
   Refreshed, I go home for hot chocolate.

4. In spring, I love to see flowers. The flowers are **blooming**.
   In spring, I love to see the blooming flowers.

5. I see the bees pollinating them. The bees are **buzzing**.
   I see the buzzing bees pollinating them.

B. **Use the participle to combine the sentences.** Possible responses:

6. In summer, I love to play in the waves at the beach. The waves are rolling.
   In summer, I love to play in the rolling waves at the beach.

7. The seagulls try to steal my food. The seagulls are diving.
   Diving, the seagulls try to steal my food.

8. I pack up and go home at the end of the day. I am tired.
   Tired, I pack up and go home at the end of the day.

9. In autumn, I love to see the colors of the leaves on the trees. The colors are changing.
   In autumn, I love to see the changing colors of the leaves on the trees.

Write It

C. **Complete each sentence to tell something that you like to do in each season. Use a participle to describe a noun or pronoun.**

10. In winter, ____.

11. In spring, ____.

12. In summer, ____.

13. In autumn, ____.

D. **(14–15) Write at least two sentences about your favorite season. Tell why you like that season. Use a participle to describe a noun or pronoun in each sentence.**

Name ______________________ Date ____________

102 What Are Participial Phrases?

Phrases That Start with a Participle

- A **phrase** is a group of related words that does not have a subject and a predicate. A **participial phrase** begins with a present **participle** or past **participle**. It describes a noun or pronoun.

  I see people **dumping garbage into the water.**
  participial phrase

  Concerned about the pollution, I think about what I can do.
  participial phrase

- Sometimes you can combine sentences by using a participial phrase. Place the participial phrase near the word that it describes. If the phrase begins a sentence, follow it with a comma (,).

  We see the factories. They **pollute the water**.
  We see the factories **polluting the water**.

  I help keep the earth unpolluted. I am **recycling paper and plastics**.
  Recycling paper and plastics, I help keep the earth unpolluted.

Try It

A. Use a participial phrase to combine the sentences. Write the new sentence. Possible responses:

1. Chemicals pollute the earth. They are seeping into the ground.
   Seeping into the ground, chemicals pollute the earth.

2. Garbage pollutes the water. Garbage is floating in the water.
   Floating in the water, garbage pollutes the water.

3. People endanger our forests. People are cutting down too many trees.
   Cutting down too many trees, people endanger our forests.

4. I see running water. It is dripping from the faucet.
   I see running water dripping from the faucet.

5. People waste our water supply. They are letting their faucets drip.
   Letting their faucets drip, people waste our water supply.

B. **Use a participial phrase to combine the sentences. Write each new sentence.** Possible responses:

6. Sometimes there are oil spills. The oil spills are caused by humans.
   Sometimes there are oil spills caused by humans.

7. This bird needs help. It has been covered by oil from the spill.
   Covered by oil from the spill, this bird needs help.

8. People are washing the bird. It has been rescued from the oily water.
   People are washing the bird rescued from the oily water.

9. The water isn't safe for seals. The water has been polluted by the spill.
   Polluted by the spill, the water isn't safe for seals.

10. This river is polluted, too. This river has been contaminated by dirty water in storm drains.
    Contaminated by dirty water in storm drains, this river is polluted, too.

11. These fish have died. They have been exposed to pollution.
    Exposed to pollution, these fish have died.

Write It

C. **Use the participial phrases in your own sentences.**

12. Tangled up in a fishing net, ______________________.

13. Made from plastic, ______________________.

14. Recycling paper, glass, and plastic, ______________________.

15. Thinking about a safe environment, ______________________.

D. **(16–20) How can people help keep the environment clean? Write at least five sentences to answer this question. Use a participial phrase in each sentence.**

____

____

____

____

____

Name ______________________ Date ____________

103 What Is a "Dangling Participle"?

It's a Participle That Describes the Wrong Word.

- Always place a **participial phrase** by the word it describes. Sometimes you can just move the phrase to fix the problem.

  Not OK: I see a rabbit **working in the garden**.

  OK: **Working in the garden**, I see a rabbit.

- Sometimes you need to rephrase the sentence and include a word for the participle to describe.

  Not OK: **Using a spade**, the holes are for my plants.

  OK: **Using a spade**, I dig holes for my plants.

Try It

A. Rewrite each sentence to fix the dangling participle. Possible responses:

1. Planting their garden, I have happy memories of my grandparents. I have happy memories of my grandparents planting their garden.

2. Thinking of my grandparents' garden, it gave me the idea to plant my own garden. Thinking of my grandparents' garden, I got the idea to plant my own garden.

3. Loving cucumbers, my garden had a lot of cucumber plants. Loving cucumbers, I planted a lot of cucumber plants.

B. Rewrite each sentence. Add a participial phrase from the box. Punctuate the new sentences carefully. Possible responses:

cut into my salad	growing on the vines	wanting my plants to grow

4. I watered them every day. Wanting my plants to grow, I watered them every day.

5. I saw tiny cucumbers. I saw tiny cucumbers growing on the vines.

6. I tasted the delicious cucumbers. I tasted the delicious cucumbers cut into my salad.

Write It

C. Answer the questions about growing food. Use a participial phrase in each answer.

7. Why do people grow their own food? ______________________________

____

8. How do people grow their own food? ______________________________

____

D. (9–12) What vegetables would you grow in your garden? Write at least four sentences. Use a participial phrase in each sentence. Check for and fix any dangling participles.

____

____

____

____

____

____

Edit It

E. (13–15) Edit this journal entry. Fix the three mistakes with dangling participles. Possible responses:

August 30

I saw one of my tomatoes turning red. I felt very impatient. Knowing that the tomatoes were ripening, ~~they gave me~~ I began to get ideas for recipes. Being very sweet, ~~I knew~~ the tomatoes would be good in a salad. Having had such a good experience this year, ~~there will definitely be~~ I will definitely plant tomatoes next year, too.

Proofreader's Marks

Delete:

Being green, ~~I knew~~ the tomatoes were not ripe.

Change text:

Wanting fresh tomatoes, ~~a garden came to mind.~~ I thought about having a garden.

See all Proofreader's Marks on page ix.

Name ______________________ Date ______________

104 Can Absolutes Help Your Writing?

Absolutely!

- An **absolute** is almost a complete sentence, but it is missing a form of the word **be**. It has a subject and a participle. An absolute relates to the entire sentence after it.

  The cool breeze tickling my face, I wake up ready for the new day.
  absolute

  The sun rising on the horizon, the day will begin soon.
  absolute

- Sometimes you can use an absolute to combine sentences and make your writing more interesting. These sentences were combined to form the sentences above.

  I wake up ready for the new day. **The cool breeze is tickling my face.**

  The day will begin soon. **The sun is rising on the horizon.**

Try It

A. Use an absolute with a present participle to combine each pair of sentences.

Possible responses:

1. I prepare for my hike. The mountain is calling to me. The mountain calling to me, I prepare for my hike.

2. The trees glitter in the sunlight. The dew is clinging to their leaves. The dew clinging to their leaves, the trees glitter in the sunlight.

3. I begin my hike. The top of the mountain is awaiting me. The top of the mountain awaiting me, I begin my hike.

B. Use an absolute with a past participle to combine each pair of sentences.

Possible responses:

4. I enjoy the view from the mountaintop. My stomach is filled from lunch. My stomach filled from lunch, I enjoy the view from the mountaintop.

5. I'm ready to hike back down. My garbage is packed in my backpack. My garbage packed in my backpack, I'm ready to hike back down.

Write It

C. Read the absolute. Then complete each sentence.

6. The deer foraging in the forest, ______________________________

______________________________.

7. The birds flying overhead, ______________________________

______________________________.

8. The mountain standing majestically behind me, ______________________________

______________________________.

D. (9–12) How do you show respect for places you visit? Write at least four sentences. Use an absolute in each sentence.

____

____

____

____

____

Edit It

E. (13–15) Edit this description. Fix the three mistakes with absolutes.

The campfire crackling in the background, I get ready to cook my dinner. The stars ~~have been~~ shining in the sky above me, I listen to the night sounds. I hear an owl hooting. Its prey ~~is~~ hiding below, the owl searches for its dinner. The lake ~~is~~ shimmering in the moonlight, the campground is quiet and peaceful.

Proofreader's Marks

Delete:

The campfire ~~is~~ crackling, my whole body feels warm.

See all Proofreader's Marks on page ix.

Name ______________________ Date ______________

105 Enrich Your Sentences

Remember: A **participle** is a verb form that can act as an adjective. A **participial phrase** begins with a participle. Participles and participial phrases describe nouns and pronouns.

- A **participle** ends in **-ing** or **-ed**, or it has a special form. It can stand alone, or it can come at the start of a **participial phrase**.

  Flowering gardens adorn the rooftop.

  Planting a garden on the rooftop, residents have made this building fun to live in.

  Ripened vegetables are ready to be picked.

  I'm eating the vegetables **grown by residents of our building**.

- You can use participial phrases to combine or expand sentences.

  Planted by all of us, the gardens are spectacular.

Try It

A. **Use a participial phrase beginning with a present participle to combine each pair of sentences. Write the new sentence.** Possible responses:

1. I am reading a report. The report describes the city of the future. I am reading a report describing the city of the future.

2. People will have gardens. The gardens will grow on rooftops. People will have gardens growing on rooftops.

3. The plants will get enough sunlight. They will be on the rooftops. Being on the rooftops, the plants will get enough sunlight.

B. **Use a participial phrase beginning with a past participle to combine each pair of sentences. Write the new sentence.** Possible responses:

4. People will not litter. They will be worried about pollution. Worried about pollution, people will not litter.

5. The city will attract residents. The city will be admired for its cleanliness. Admired for its cleanliness, the city will attract residents.

Write It

C. Expand the sentences with participial phrases. Write the new sentences.

6. I want to move to the city. ______________________________

____

7. The city has a lot to offer people like me. ______________________________

____

D. (8–12) What would your perfect city of the future be like? Write at least five sentences. Use participial phrases in each sentence.

____

____

____

____

____

____

Edit It

E. (13–15) Improve this letter. Add three participial phrases that describe the underlined words. Possible responses:

Dear Uncle Carl,

Being someone who loves city life, I am really enjoying this city. I am spending a lot of time ^visiting museums. This is a really clean city. The people here do not throw trash on the streets. It is pleasant to walk along the streets ^filled with flowers instead of trash. ^Surrounded by so many shops, I am doing a lot of shopping, too!

Love,

Elizabeth

Proofreader's Marks

Add text:
^Impressed by the cleanliness, Elizabeth wants to move to this city.

See all Proofreader's Marks on page ix.